THEODORE SHACKLEY

THE
THIRD
OPTION

*An American View of
Counterinsurgency
Operations*

Reader's Digest Press

McGraw-Hill Book Company

NEW YORK   ST. LOUIS   SAN FRANCISCO
HAMBURG   MEXICO   TORONTO

1 2 3 4 5 6 7 8 9 F G F G 8 7 6 5 4 3 2 1

LIBRARY OF CONGRESS CATALOGING IN PUBLICATION DATA

Shackley, Theodore.
The third option.
Bibliography: p.
Includes index.
1. Counterinsurgency—Case studies.   2. World
politics—1975-1985.   3. World politics—1965-1975.
4. United States—Military policy.   I. Title.
U241.S43   355'.02184'0926   80-26947
ISBN 0-07-056382-9

CONTENTS

This book is dedicated to the heroic Meo hill tribes of North Laos. I hope it will bring some small recognition to a nomadic, freedom-loving people who fought the full military power of North Vietnam to a standstill. Under the leadership of their general, Vang Pao, the Meo used counterinsurgency techniques to fight a war of position and maneuver in North Laos from 1961 to 1973. But the fruits of their battlefield victories were ultimately lost to Hanoi's puppets, the Pathet Lao, in the political arena. This tragedy does not detract, however, from the Meo's contributions for a decade to the purposes of the kingdom of Laos and the United States.

Battlefield realities in South Vietnam and political disquiet at home forced the United States in 1975 to abandon its long-standing commitment to a neutral, but independent, Laos. Although they were skilled practitioners of irregular warfare, the Meo could not withstand Hanoi's assault when their primary ally, the United States, had lost the political will to sustain them in their battle for survival. Thousands of Meo fled Laos. But those who have found temporary physical safety in neighboring Thailand are far from secure. Hanoi's use of naked military power in its pursuit of dominance over all of Indochina is clear to all of us.

A lesson rings loud and clear from America's experience with the Meo: Our policy makers must evaluate the cost of indecisiveness and weakness in human terms. In the past this lesson has not been applied. It must be in the future if the United States is to repolish its tarnished reputation for honoring commitments to those who struggle to maintain independence from those who would conquer the free.

ACKNOWLEDGMENTS

I am not alone. Since 1976—and the election of President Jimmy Carter—approximately 2,800 American career intelligence officers like myself have retired, many of them prematurely. They were a national treasure—their experience in intelligence, counterintelligence, and counterinsurgency spanned decades. These men and women were professionals. Their expertise and dedication were unquestioned. They have not boasted of their accomplishments; they are true to their oaths of silence. They deserve more than a warm handshake when they walk through the doors of the Central Intelligence Agency's headquarters at Langley, Virginia, into retirement and the outside world.

In the post-Watergate and -Vietnam era, the CIA was accused of a shocking variety of ugly deeds: It was a shadow government run amok; a nest of fascists existed in Langley; its people were assassins, and worse. Under the harsh glare of public scrutiny, they were undressed, item by item, until they stood naked. Allies and enemies alike were quick to take stock. In Europe, a major foreign intelligence service suddenly became reluctant to "source" its own intelligence reports to us. And for good reason. Who could say that their secret "assets" might not become fodder for open committee discussion in Washington? The word was out: open season on the CIA.

Within our own society, some of those we were charged with protecting took the opportunity to neutralize us further. Manipulating such tools as the Freedom of Information Act and vested freedom, they went so far as actually to publish names and addresses of CIA officers based in our embassies abroad. This was a contributing factor in the murder of one of them. Even worse, it undermined our credibility with those nations that counted upon our eyes and ears. The real loser, of course, was America. It was not unlike watching someone busily sawing at his own wrists with a dull razor blade. Ultimately the veins began to bleed.

A lackluster performance by the CIA was in part responsible for the presence of a Soviet combat brigade in Cuba. Our on-again, off-again commitment to pro-Western forces in Angola made us a laugh-

Acknowledgments

ingstock. The overthrow of the Shah of Iran—a long-time ally and critical source of stability in the Persian Gulf—found us with our pants around our ankles. We were shocked by the seizure of our diplomats—even though the Tehran Embassy had already been a target for one attack. In our own hemisphere, Nicaragua was taken over by pro-Cuban revolutionaries. And tiny El Salvador teeters on the brink. And capping it all is the humiliating failure of the United States either to predict or to respond meaningfully to the Soviet invasion of Afghanistan.

My dilemma was painfully clear. How could a citizen—a career intelligence officer at that—convey to a broad audience some of the concerns that foreign policy specialists have about what the United States *should* do to meet foreign policy challenges of the 1980s? How could the United States project power into distant lands, thus restoring some control over events which threaten our very survival? This issue has long preoccupied intelligence officers, particularly since the trauma of a lost Vietnam forced senior officials to retreat into a narrow, unimaginative range of choices in considering such foreign policy options.

I found that retirement offered me the luxury to think about America's choice of policy options and a balanced intelligence collection capability for the 1980s in a way that I could not while I was on active federal service. My concepts—and concerns—which emerged from mature reflection were tested by research in public libraries and by discussions with politicians, journalists, diplomats, military officers, policemen, businessmen, and nongovernmental experts from the United States and abroad on intelligence, counterintelligence, counterinsurgency, and covert action techniques. Meanwhile, private sources such as research institutes in Europe were a gold mine of factual data on insurgent movements which threaten world security today. I am indebted to all* who contributed so generously of their knowledge and time to make the views outlined in this book possible.

The responsibility for interpreting what I learned rests solely with me—and errors, therefore, of fact or interpretation that may mar this work must be charged to the author. I have tried to distill overt information clinically, objectively, and from perspectives generally unavailable to the public by applying to the intelligence problems of the 1980s my experience as a professional intelligence officer who for twenty-eight years countered threats that will ever more fiercely beset the United States in the coming decades as it struggles to survive.

Make no mistake. We—all of us—*are* locked in a struggle for survival. And naïveté only increases the odds which have steadily mounted against us in the past five years. A simple belief in the righteousness of our cause in not enough. Right does not necessarily make might. Ask the Poles. Ask the Czechs.

---

*This manuscript has been reviewed by the Publication Review Board of the Central Intelligence Agency to assist the author in eliminating classified information.

Acknowledgments

Ask the Hungarians. Ask the Meo of Laos. And write their answers as epitaphs.

Year by year, nation by nation, we have relinquished our ability to shape events throughout the world. This abdication of global responsibility has created vast power vacuums—if not ours, then someone else's. The challenge is unmistakably clear: Do we influence our own destiny and survival in the turbulent 1980s—or do others who, I assure you, mean us no goodwill? Our options in dealing with this dilemma are painfully few.

At one end there is the give-and-take through the normal channels of negotiation and diplomacy; at the other lies the unthinkable: war. But there is yet one more.

Experts in revolutionary warfare and paramilitary operations call it the third option.

THE THIRD OPTION

CHAPTER I

THE CHALLENGE

As the decade of the 1980s opens, Cuban mercenary armies sustain dictatorial governments in two large African nations, Angola and Ethiopia. In our own hemisphere, Cuban- and Soviet-trained revolutionaries rule in Nicaragua, and threaten to seize neighboring El Salvador. In the Middle East—a larder for survival of the Western world—the southern tip of the Arabian peninsula has become an armed camp for the military forces of the Soviet Union and its allies. From this base they have attacked and intimidated North Yemen and pose today a threat to an eastern neighbor, Oman, the country that controls the straits of the Persian Gulf through which more than half the free world's oil supply moves in giant, vulnerable tankers at the rate of one every fifteen minutes.

A Soviet army has all but conquered Afghanistan only three hundred miles away from these vital straits. Meanwhile, the nation in between, Iran, is racked by revolution, drifting toward disintegration, and is at war with Iraq. Farther east, beyond the Bay of Bengal, the Soviet-supported armies of North Vietnam are rooting out native resistance in Laos and Cambodia and are menacing Thailand.

These, then, are only areas where Communist-trained and -supported forces are engaged in open combat. Elsewhere—such as in Guatemala, Honduras, and Zaire—Soviet-supported guerrilla movements are arming and training, waiting for the moment to pounce on weak or isolated governments. What business, some may ask, is this of ours—of the Americans?

Take a map of the world. Trace the vital supply routes and key passages through which naval forces must proceed to the critical theaters of potential conflict. Note the vital oil routes from Venezuela to the United States, the location of the Panama Canal in relation to Nicaragua and Cuba. Note the small nations, impoverished and politically unstable, that line the shores and, as islands, dot the face of the Caribbean. How many of them are increasingly under Castro's influence?

Now gaze across the Atlantic to the Strait of Gibraltar, gateway to the Mediterranean and North Africa. Only a great effort by the democratic parties in

The Challenge

Portugal and their friends in the Western world fought off the Soviet Union's drive in 1974 to establish a Communist government there. Down the oil-rich west coast of Africa there is a string of small states, insecure and uncertain of the future, that waiver in and out of alliance with the Soviet Union. Beyond them are Angola with its Cuban garrison and Namibia, another target of Soviet-trained insurgents.

Then go east to the Indian Ocean. There, at the "choke point," the narrowing southern end of the Red Sea—the oven of Bab el Mandeb—lies the "People's Democratic Republic of Yemen." Formerly the British-run Aden Protectorate and home of Britain's Middle East strike force, it has been converted to a Soviet naval base, as well as a training and staging area for armed forces and terrorists from many Soviet-dominated countries and NATO members like West Germany. Across the strait lies Ethiopia, deep within the Horn of Africa, a large and ancient land now firmly under the control of Soviet and Cuban troops. Now run your finger back across the Red Sea. North of Soviet-controlled South Yemen—bordering on Saudi Arabia—is the Yemen Arab Republic, the most populous state on the Arabian peninsula. It is home for a million or more workers now living in Saudi Arabia. South Yemeni assassins have killed two North Yemeni presidents. Last year South Yemen attacked its neighbors to the north with Soviet- and Cuban-supplied and -advised forces. Intimidated by South Yemen and uncertain of Saudi or Western support, North Yemen seems to be knuckling under to the South Yemeni—and, behind them, the Soviet Union.

Skip now to the heat-blasted wastes of Saudi Arabia and the timeless sands of the Rub al Khali—the dread Empty Quarter. Follow the track of the ancient spice caravans where they moved centuries ago up the western coast of the Persian Gulf to the Soviet Union's ally, Iraq. Beyond Iraq to the east is Iran, where Soviet influence is growing, and then still farther east—on the opposite side of the gulf now—is Afghanistan, where Soviet troops and planes are breaking the resistance of a fiercely independent people with tanks and chemical warfare agents. But do not stop here. Look eastward still, past Pakistan and India and the temples of Mandalay to the peninsula of Indochina. Here the warrior Communists of Vietnam are near their goal of ruling it all. Thailand and Malaysia may well be next.

Is there a pattern to all this? Unless one can eavesdrop on the plans of the Kremlin, one cannot say. But the proximity of "revolutionary states" and major Soviet-supported insurgent movements to key choke points and trade routes is at best suspicious, at worst a terrifying coincidence. Is the encirclement of Saudi Arabia and the gulf happenstance? A prudent leader would say no—for he could not afford to agree.

We can be sure of only one thing: Soviet-supported nations and insurgencies are increasingly clustered in areas of critical importance to the survival of the United States. The fateful chain of events which led to this may have links that reach back into the histories of the nations involved, but the actual threat to our interests is the product of the last few years—the same years during which the United States, as a matter of policy, abandoned the use of covert means to support its friends and then turned away from opportunities to help its sympathizers in countering insurgent movements. A coincidence? Once again, a prudent man would answer with care.

Since the age of steam and steel, no nation has been able to hide within a shrinking world. Nor can a great power avoid the responsibilities of its position. If a nation forswears the use of power to protect its allies and interests, then it misuses that power as surely as if it employed force for brutal aggression. During much of the last two decades Americans have been caught in a dilemma. What is our role in the world—our national destiny? How do we weigh these against reality? Some say we should disdain the use of power abroad—come what may—because it is inherently immoral. Self-interest? Or is it simply self-expression? If so, well, the world is not listening.

Granted our recognition of what is good versus that which is evil, the wise use of the power of the state is unavoidably necessary for our own national security and the survival of the free and bountiful civilization that we and the nations with which we have joined in alliance have created. Thus, whether we like it or not, our Western civilization remains the most attractive example of a way of life to the majority of people all over the world. Despite the vehemence of propaganda attacks by hostile governments, the best evidence is that it remains the lodestone for mankind's aspirations.

One result of national debate over the past years has been a change in attitudes toward a flexible use of power involving means other than diplomacy, trade, or open military force. But no successful state in history has limited its activities solely to these. Only one, to my knowledge, has ever tried—the United States in the past few years. In times of peril all nations seek whatever means they can find to preserve themselves. In time of peace Thomas Jefferson, for one, used deception and secrecy to effect the greatest single act of foreign policy in our history, the purchase of the Louisiana Territory, outside of prescribed channels and in direct violation of our Constitution. And our purchase of Alaska—as far as Russia is concerned today—was a rip-off. Should we give it back? Shall we poll Alaskans? These, then, are all facets to what irregular warfare technocrats call—for better or worse—the third option to the persuasions of diplomacy and trade on the one hand and military force on the other. It also includes all aspects of covert action, which in some lexicons is defined as the influencing of people and the shaping of events through the use of political, economic or military factors, without the sponsor of this activity being identified in an attributable manner. Covert action is an intelligence discipline which can be subdivided into several functional parts, one such seg-

The Challenge

ment being paramilitary operations or the furnishing of *covert* military assistance to unconventional and conventional foreign forces and organizations. This means, depending on which side of a conflict the United States is on, it can be devoted to either fostering or defeating so-called "revolutionary wars." Thus, the paramilitary aspect of the third option can be used in support of offensive or guerrilla warfare operations. It can also be harnessed in counterinsurgency operations, which are defensive in nature. As the 1980s are likely to be a decade in which the United States will be reacting to challenges, much like a counterpunching boxer, it has been assumed our irregular warfare concerns will focus on combating "armed clandestine organizations" whose primary goal is to impose their will on the population in the countries where they are attempting to seize power. This book has concentrated, therefore, on the counterinsurgency part of paramilitary operations. None of the techniques of covert action or paramilitary operations are substitutes for policy. They are not panaceas. They are, collectively, an option. Uncontrolled, they can confuse and even distort a democratic country like the United States. Although I know of no instance in our history when the institutions of government dedicated to covert action have been so used, there have been such cases in other countries: France in its struggle with Algeria over the latter's independence is a textbook case where government-sponsored covert action programs were diverted by military officers from assigned tasks to new targets which were French political personalities or parties. Admiral Canaris, the head of military intelligence (Abwher) in Germany during World War II, certainly tried to use the covert action resources at his service's disposal to alter Adolf Hitler's conduct of the war.

Much has been written in recent years about the incompatibility of the role of a secret intelligence service with the mores of an open society. But as a matter of clear historical record, *democratic societies* have, over the centuries, employed secret services with no noticeable ill effects on free institutions.

Effective intelligence services and covert action campaigns have played decisive roles in the preservation of free nations under attack by insurgents and foreign agents. In the immediate post-World War II era Greece, Italy, and the Philippines received life support through clandestine means or direct paramilitary assistance to help defeat forces dedicated to the overthrow of the government. Malaysia and Singapore came somewhat later. In almost every case the Soviet Union and other Communist countries significantly abetted the insurgents.

Soviet-backed insurgencies are the final arguments favoring America's need to conduct and maintain competence in covert action and counterinsurgency in response to this challenge, for quite clearly the Kremlin has dedicated itself to expanding its influence and dominion over others through clandestine means. It should hardly be news.

In 1915, for example, pacifists and radicals from all over continental Europe met in Switzerland to protest the continuation of the First World War. Among those present was Vladimir Lenin, then in exile from czarist Russia. One of the pacifists, noting Lenin's absence from a meeting, went to find him. The man finally ran Lenin and some of his comrades to ground in a forest—and was shocked to find him practicing with firearms. The truth can often be ugly. Lenin, his supporters, and their legatees—the Bolsheviks who formed the Communist Party of the Soviet Union—have been preoccupied with the use of force and camouflage from their beginnings. And over the years, the tools of political warfare—propaganda, deception, "agents of influence," bribery, and secret financial support—have been used to advance and protect Soviet interests in both developed countries and the third world whenever other means were tactically inappropriate. Where the situation requires it (often as a result of the successful application of the methods just mentioned), the Soviets have turned to more direct means: the fostering of insurgency and guerrilla warfare and outright invasion.

Since the founding of the Comintern in 1919, the Soviet Union has provided schools and training programs, financial and operational support, and refuge for revolutionaries, terrorists, and insurgents whose activities further its interests. An acceleration of this program over the last decade has resulted in the buildup of a vast apparatus from the Soviet Union and among its allies, such as South Yemen, to support insurgencies and subversion. Each year this apparatus has assessed the usefulness of thousands of foreign visitors—many of them students—to the

Communist cause. Promising recruits are trained in marksmanship, sabotage, use of explosives, survival in the bush, political agitation and indoctrination, secret communications, and other techniques of clandestine operations. A principal conduit for these terrorists and guerrillas-in-waiting is Patrice Lumumba University in Moscow, which accepts more than 1,000 students a year from Asia, Africa, and Latin America. Traditionally the assistant dean of Lumumba University is a high-ranking Soviet staff intelligence officer. The entire faculty is virtually composed of intelligence officers whose principal function is to spot and screen potential supporters for Soviet interests, be they political, intelligence, or paramilitary operations. There is, of course, much chaff with the wheat in this process. The chaff is given some kind of education and then sent home, while the wheat is carefully cultivated, nurtured, and trained for Soviet purposes.

Through this process, the Soviets developed Illich Ramírez, known the world over as Carlos, the assassin and terrorist who, among other exploits, organized the kidnapping of the Organization of Petroleum Exporting Countries (OPEC) leaders in 1975. It was hardly a shock that Carlos spent a year at Lumumba University. In his second year, however, he suddenly announced his "disillusionment" with the Soviet system and disappeared from view. Not long afterward he surfaced, working with an extremist Arab terrorist organization, and proceeded on his bloody trail. Although it is perhaps too gener-

The Challenge

ous to ascribe all the killings and kidnappings engineered by Carlos to Soviet inspiration, he and his associates have clearly been encouraged and supported in crucial ways by the KGB and other Soviet-controlled organizations. For example, Carlos used a Soviet antiaircraft rocket launcher (SA-7) in Paris in an attempt to shoot down an Israeli passenger jet. In 1973 his cell received explosives from Bulgaria. In Paris he conspired with Henri Curiel—an Egyptian Jew who was a Communist with links to the French Communist Party, the KGB, and the Cuban Dirección General de Inteligencia (DGI)—and ran a support organization for terrorists in general.

Ulrike Meinhof, the German assassin and terrorist, was a Communist Party member. So was her husband, the publisher of a West German exposé and sex magazine subsidized by Communist funds supplied from Prague. Nor have allies of the Soviet Union hesitated in supplying arms, training facilities, and money to international terrorists and potential insurgents like the Baader-Meinhof gang in West Germany. George Habash, the leader of the extreme Palestinian terrorist organization, the Popular Front for the Liberation of Palestine (PFLP), is but one recipient of financial largess from, among others, East Germany and North Korea. East Germany also furnishes training sites for such groups; Czechoslovakia adds money and arms.

A former Cuban intelligence officer, Orlando Castro Hidalgo, has testified that in the early 1960s some 1,500 men a year were brought to Cuba for training from other parts of the world. They were given a three- to six-month course and sometimes as long as a year in guerrilla warfare. In 1967 Manuel Carrasquel, a Venezuelan, told of training in Cuba at Camp Matanzas, one of *three* such camps near Havana. A chief professor was none other than General Viktor Simenov of the Soviet KGB, who was simultaneously moonlighting as chief of operations for the Cuban intelligence service.[1]

The role of the Soviet Union in manipulating and frustrating the policies of other governments through foreign-based Communist parties and through its intelligence services is as old as the country itself. British historian E. H. Carr, for example, once noted that "the initiative in introducing propaganda as a regular instrument of international relations must be credited to the Soviet government. . . . Soviet Russia was the first national unit to preach an international doctrine and maintain an effective world propaganda organization."[2] Other countries have attempted to follow this lead, but only the Soviet Union could marshal such diverse organizations and "fronts" as the Women's International Democratic Federation, the Maison du Livre Étranger, and the Japanese Friends of the Russian Language Association to advance the policies of one particular state.

---

[1]Christopher Dobson and Ronald Payne, *The Carlos Complex* (New York: G. P. Putnam, 1977), p. 33.

[2]Edward H. Carr, *The Bolshevik Revolution 1917–1923* (New York: Macmillan Company, 1951), vol. 1, pp. 137–138.

The Challenge

Failure to confront and repel the challenge posed by these techniques of international political warfare is dangerous, recklessly so. Indeed, such failure might well lead ultimately to a nuclear confrontation between the Soviet Union, controlling much of the world, and an isolated, embattled United States, turning to its nuclear arsenal in convulsive desperation.

In fact, Kremlinologists say this is pretty much the way the Soviets see the possibility of nuclear war. But we still have the option to combat expanding Soviet influence through political warfare and counterinsurgency so that the balance of world power—the Soviets call it the correlation of forces—is never so favorable as to lead them to the ultimate temptation . . . or us to the ultimate desperation.

Political warfare is very often the stitch in time that eliminates bloodier and more costly alternatives. There are cases in which a cause supported, a newspaper campaign initiated, or a particular candidate encouraged in an election could mean (and in the past has meant) that the crisis in which our vital interests might be at stake never arises. Such comparatively minor preventive actions are likely to be most effective when heavy-handed Soviet efforts to influence events in an area are already obvious—and frequently as discreet and delicate as a jackhammer.

But beyond the goal of defusing a crisis lies the broader strategic aim of trying to influence the Soviet Union itself. A new Russia, open to the world, with an authentically representative government would be much more likely to contribute to a resolution of the grave problems that mankind faces. Here political action can do little unless it is a coordinated policy that seeks to establish coherence on all aspects of our operations that touch the Soviet Union. To be most effective, such a coordinated policy should include such passive weapons as trade, cultural, and academic exchanges. Most are not secret or devious, but their effectiveness can be devastating when guided and coordinated by a professional political action cadre which understands the Soviet Union and its weaknesses and insecurities. There is no myopia in the Kremlin. It spends enormous amounts of money, time, and effort to influence the views and policies of our nation. Should we not seize any reasonable opportunity to try, directly or indirectly, openly or secretly, to influence theirs?

Like it or not, we must engage in political or covert action if we are to defend ourselves effectively against international terrorism, which strikes today at the very foundations of civilization itself. For centuries, even the most primitive nations recognized that it was in their own self-interest that diplomatic representatives be assured personal immunity and security. No longer. The assassinations and abductions of diplomats imperil this heretofore sacrosanct tradition. This development eats like rust at the ability of nations to conduct civilized relations with each other and forces the transfer of resources from productive pursuits to economically nonproductive defenses. Most alarming, it jeopardizes the liberty and safety of the innocent while disrupting social order, the basis for freedom, which government exists to uphold. Beyond such horizons lurk chaos and anarchy. As an alternative, the third option is hardly a Hobson's choice. It is common sense.

An essential element of the third option is penetration of the enemy organization—that is, having your own agent inside the enemy camp. (Knowing what a terrorist group plans to do, you can do something about it.) Guards, burglar alarms, and watchdogs cannot do all that much to prevent the tragedies that the Carloses of the world would inflict upon us, nor do they help bring them to justice. For this you need informants or, more crudely, spies. To recruit such "assets," as they are also known, you must build an organization capable of protecting secret operations, policed by only a few responsible officials, who themselves are isolated on a "need to know" basis. Finally, if you are at all serious, you must arm that organization with the power and legal authority to neutralize the terrorist bands uncovered. Nothing complicated here: ABC common sense.

Counterterrorism also demands an effective and deceptive "mix" of covert actions to keep bandit nations, such as Libya or Cuba, off-balance—thus less able to breed, nest, and nurture terrorists. Nations which sponsor terrorist intervention in the internal affairs of other countries (Libya's assistance to IRA gunmen, for just one example) surely should not be immune from external efforts to persuade them to mend their homicidal ways. Such enlightened covert actions can also assist third world countries in effecting constructive socioeconomic changes which deny terrorists a cause.

Probably the most effective form of covert action is the clandestine sponsorship of armed insurgency and its antidote, counterinsurgency. Insurgencies—the Russians call them "wars of national liberation"—and the methods of combating them constitute the principal subject of this book. All my professional experience convinces me that given the character of the worldwide assault now being mounted against us, we must first of all understand the nature of insurgencies, then, on the most urgent national basis, swiftly rebuild our capability to combat them.

To understand how this capability has deteriorated, we need only look back briefly to 1975, when the United States turned its back and ran away from two major challenges. Much of our present baleful quandary about the conduct of foreign affairs largely originated in that period. Would the "militants" who stormed our embassy in Tehran have done so had they· not seen on television the brawling evacuation of our embassy in Saigon? Would there be close to 100,000 troops from Communist countries in Africa today if the United States had not refused, by congressional action, to help the non-Communist guerrillas in Angola, in Somalia—anywhere in the globe? Would American "commitment" have become an entertaining locker-room joke among allies and opponents alike?

The Challenge

After the debacle in Vietnam, a humiliated U.S. foreign policy establishment blushed and turned its attention elsewhere to what it felt to be safe turf. Military planners concentrated on rebuilding the conventional army, strengthening NATO, and sorting through the murky implications of the Strategic Arms Limitation Talks. Attention shifted from "wars of national liberation"—Communist-sponsored insurgencies—to what is euphemistically referred to as "essential equivalence" of strategic forces between the United States and the Soviet Union. Thus mesmerized, we forgot how the Soviet Union defined détente for the third world: "... to extend *détente* to Asia, Africa and Latin America ..., it was necessary to step up the fight against imperialist intrigue, to abolish the hotbeds of colonialism and racism, to extinguish the existing military conflicts."[3]

During this period of paralytic hand wringing and self-examination the debate about which options the United States should have available to deal with crises abroad took place, in both public forums and congressional hearings. Before Congress, William Colby, then CIA director, accurately summed up the dilemma in which we had locked ourselves. He said the nation had two options short of a nuclear confrontation in coping with international crises: We could send in the marines, we could do nothing. Senior intelligence officers like myself, who had experience in paramilitary operations, had always insisted that the United States should also consider the

[3]Oleg Orestov, "Cohesion of the Forces of Peace and Progress," *Soviet Military Review,* vol. 11 (November 1976), pp. 55–56.

third option: the use of guerrilla warfare, counterinsurgency techniques and covert action to achieve policy goals. In our view, irregular warfare skills would give the United States an additional arrow in its national defense quiver.

Those who listened generally acknowledged that our experience over nearly two decades in such diverse areas as Cuba, the Dominican Republic, Vietnam, Laos, Cambodia, the Philippines, Zaire, and Angola proved that we understood how to combat "wars of national liberation." We had also shown how potent an offensive weapon guerrillas like the Meo of Laos could be when their courage, mobility and superior knowledge of terrain were linked to the destructive firepower of tactical aircraft that were flown to support their operations. But the trauma of Vietnam had left the nation's leaders unwilling to use either guerrilla warfare or counterinsurgency techniques. When the Ford administration attempted in November 1975 to use irregular warfare measures to prevent an easy victory in the Angolan civil war by Soviet-backed Cuban forces, Congress, via the Tunney amendment, forbade expenditure of *any* funds in Angola—except to gather intelligence. Thus, the United States chose to do nothing when confronted with the need to project power in a distant land—and by so doing awarded Cuban interference with not only a victory but a springboard base from which to launch other adventures in Africa.

The clear lessons of Angola did not make many

converts for paramilitary operations among either members of the executive branch or Congress. Instead, the third option became even more unpopular, distasteful. Despite this, advocates of counterinsurgency have continued to argue that it is likely United States interests will be ever more widely challenged through "wars of national liberation." They predicted that Moscow, Havana, and, in some areas, Beijing would exploit the impatience for reform which lies just below the surface in much of Latin America, Africa, the Middle East, and Southeast Asia. Others, equally articulate and at the same time politically more influential, argued differently—and shrilly: The United States has no right to interfere in the internal affairs of other sovereign states, they insisted, no matter what the provocation or danger. Unlike Isaac Newton, who discovered new dimensions of gravity by waiting for an apple to drop from a tree, they simply sat beneath the boughs and said "ouch" when hit.

Until now their view has prevailed. Not surprising, then, that although Presidents Ford and Carter directed the United States to maintain a counterinsurgency capability, this capability has withered into virtual uselessness. We at CIA knew it. And we knew our enemies and allies knew we knew it—yet we did nothing. Budgetary pressures, particularly under Admiral Stansfield Turner's stewardship of the intelligence community, forced drastic personnel reductions and maintained equipment inventories at levels below what I believe are necessary to sustain the third option—if it were selected for implementation. In my view, it would take at least three years to train a new cadre of guerrilla warfare and counterinsurgency experts. An expansion of the weapons inventory and other supplies could be done in less time—and at a minimum cost of about $6 million. But the fact remains that we now have less irregular warfare and counterinsurgency capability than our vital national interests demand.

While the United States lodges complaints with the United Nations, the Soviet Union supports revolutionary groups with *deeds* as well as words. In the Soviet lexicon "words" translate into propaganda support and "deeds" into provision of arms, funds, and training for guerrillas.

Beyond shrinking reserves of skills and weapons, we have also given up the concept of "plausible denial." It almost seems that Congress and the press want to insist that we publicly announce any covert action even before it begins. Perhaps there is something especially moral about playing poker with your back to a mirror, but it isn't profitable. In contrast, a closed Soviet society permits "plausible denial" to flourish and makes it easier for the Soviets to work with guerrilla movements via intermediaries. Even our allies do not mislead themselves. In Britain—a nation which is the model for democracies across the world—the government imposes censorship on a free press when it is about to publish a story deemed against the national security. This process is called the issuance of a D Notice. Such self-serving devices appear to horrify many Americans who seem to be motivated more by self-expression than self-interest. Do as I do, and I shall kiss you. Not so the Soviets.

The Kremlin recognizes that insurgents are usually found in the early phases of their development in remote, often inaccessible rural areas. On-the-scene presence of Soviet personnel in such regions could generate suspicion and thus risk dropping the disguise of a "strictly national" insurgency. Therefore, the Soviets apply subtle camouflage. They employ others to do what needs to be done to assist the insurgents. Their true role is hidden. They can deny the use of guerrillas as an instrument of national policy. Cuba is the Soviet Union's favorite Trojan horse—and it is so overworked it has become both battle scarred and war weary. Some of its people must wonder, therefore, if selling sugar and rum in world markets wouldn't be more profitable than exporting revolutions. Occasionally, East Germany and North Korea also serve as Soviet stalking horses.

For years the Soviet attitude toward guerrilla groups was rigid. The Soviets supported only those groups that they could control. This view changed with realization that havoc caused by autononous guerrilla and terrorist groups in unstable parts of the world often paid off in handsome bonuses—even *if* unplanned and uncontrolled by the Soviet Union. Such disorder and chaos sapped funds and energy away from more constructive social or economic reforms which would undercut the whole reason for the insurgency to begin with. As a result, in the mid-1960s the KGB started aiding guerrilla groups that were not necessarily Moscow's willing lackeys.

Take the experience of Vladimir Nikolaevich Sakharov, a KGB agent prior to his defection in Kuwait in July 1971, as outlined by John Barron, the American author and acknowledged expert on the KGB.[4] It clearly illustrates the new Soviet outlook. In early 1970 Sakharov learned that both the KGB and the Soviet military intelligence service, the Chief Intelligence Directorate (GRU), were exploiting Palestinian guerrillas. By that summer he had read intelligence reports which showed that the KGB was smuggling weapons to the Palestine Liberation Organization (PLO) via Egypt. He also learned that the GRU, the intelligence arm of the Soviet army, was providing guerrilla warfare training in the Soviet Union to select Palestinian candidates. (Brian Crozier, former director of the London-based Institute for the Study of Conflict, confirms the existence of a GRU sabotage and insurgency school in the Crimea. His information also indicates that black African guerrillas from South Africa and Namibia have been trained in camps outside Odessa.)

Furthermore, Sakharov revealed that the Soviets carefully avoided involvement with Palestinian airline hijacking operations, fearful that their own clandestine links to the PLO might surface in the

[4]Interview with John Barron, author of the book *KGB, The Secret Work of Soviet Agents* (New York: The Reader's Digest Press, 1974) in Washington, D.C., on January 7, 1980, concerning Soviet support to guerrilla and terrorist groups.

aftermath and debris of a failure. On May 10, 1971, this fear prompted the Central Committee to issue a top-secret directive to Soviet embassies to keep the Palestinians at arm's length.[5] Contacts were to be handled only by the KGB and the GRU and through the Soviet Afro-Asian Solidarity Committee—a KGB front organization. Their support of Palestinian terrorists, in my judgment, has been massive. Since 1974 about 1,000 Palestinians have received Soviet training in guerrilla warfare in the Soviet Union, East Germany, and Czechoslovakia. And roughly two-thirds of all the guerrillas and terrorists trained in the Soviet Union or Eastern Europe are from Fatah, the PLO's main military branch.

Despite heavy camouflage, Soviet-sponsored "wars of national liberation" have been exposed in such diverse locations as Chad, Lebanon, Namibia, Oman, South Africa, Sudan, Thailand, and Zimbabwe. This dangerous magnitude of involvement with insurgencies must be understood by Americans who shape or influence our policy. If, however, doubts remain about the nature of this challenge, the skeptic should examine the new "Brezhnev" constitution of the USSR. Chapter IV, Article 28 states: "The Soviet Union is committed to strengthening the position of world socialism, of supporting the struggles of peoples for national liberation and social progress." The message is blunt and its implications are clear.

[5] John Barron, *KGB: The Secret Work of Soviet Secret Agents* (New York: The Reader's Digest Press, 1974), p. 57.

Despite ideological differences with the Soviet Union on many issues, the People's Republic of China is as deeply committed to the exploitation of "wars of national liberation" for security purposes as is Moscow. Historically China has been preoccupied with the need to defend its borders and extend its influence over legitimate spheres of interests. This explains Beijing's long-standing commitment to insurgencies in Burma, Thailand, Malaysia, and Cambodia. Chinese support generally follows the Soviet pattern: plausible denial, while providing arms, ammunition, training, funds, and propaganda aid. On occasion the Chinese stray from their regional role and participate in insurgencies as far away as Angola, where they backed the anti-Soviet group led by Jonas Savimbi. Generally, however, the Chinese are less adventurous than the Soviets. China's limited ability to deliver supplies to far-off places undoubtedly makes for caution.

For the rest of this century the third option is likely to become more important for the United States than in the past. Major Soviet political initiatives in Europe, such as its successful campaign against the enhanced radiation shell (the so-called neutron bomb) and the current attack on intermediate-range nuclear weapons for Western Europe, will probably increase. We should be willing and able to help those in Western Europe who favor a strong defense to combat these well-financed and massively staffed drives. Countering terrorism is also a growing concern in Europe, and the Europeans' no-nonsense efforts to curb it are far better than our own. Indeed, America's tactics are not unlike those of a sapper who attempts to locate land mines by trodding gently on the terrain—with earplugs in case of an explosion.

It is, however, in the Near East, Africa, Latin America, and Asia that covert action, especially guerrilla warfare and counterinsurgency, may make crucial differences in the success or failure of Western policies.

Vanishing raw materials, coupled with increasing population and social, economic, and political upheavals, will add to the instability of many developing countries. Soviet interests in these areas are simple: Exclude the Western powers from some; establish military bases directly or through surrogates like the Cubans in others; exercise dominant political influence; and establish control of major natural resources where they exist. The vulnerability of our oil supply in the Middle East is hardly the world's best-kept secret. Now something new has been added. According to recently released CIA reports, the Soviet Union and its East European satellites will soon need some of that oil for themselves. The cost and difficulty of developing the USSR's Siberian reserves in the next decade make access to Middle East oil of great importance. For a country whose commercial exports are as competitive as an icebox on the Arctic Circle, but whose ability in subversion and intrigue is unsurpassed, the logic of the situation seems clear. If Soviet control over Afghanistan is established, we may expect to see "popular liberation forces" in Pakistan's Baluchistan and Pashtunistan. The Soviets might even succeed in seizing control, indirectly, in the minority areas of Iran while their Tudeh party in Tehran takes over during the chaos of national disintegration. (As we contemplate what is happening in Iran today, we should remember that for more than twenty-five years, since the CIA-assisted coup of 1953, Iran was the major stabilizing force in the Middle East—an example to others of land reform, public health and education, industrial development, and the emancipation of women.)

When we examine the world today, we see nations on every continent embattled by Communist-trained, if not always Communist-inspired, movements dedicated to the disruption of public order and, at the least, the breakdown of the normal processes of government. These nations—many are old allies—face incipient revolution. Others are undergoing the terror of civil war: Namibia, Cambodia, Iran, and El Salvador. And one country, Afghanistan, where the right kind of help might *still* count, is being brutalized by an invader in the name of social progress. The best possible American covert action, guerrilla warfare, and counterinsurgency teams could not have saved the day everywhere. But there is an undeniable parallel between the recent collapse of our competence in these fields and the spread of instability and insurgency throughout many parts of the globe. The time has come to test whether this

The Challenge

tragic trend can be reversed and whether a renewal of the third option can help stem and then turn the flooding tide.

In succeeding chapters I have outlined and illustrated the stages through which insurgencies evolve through contemporary examples. Simultaneously, I have tried to explain and illustrate the armory of techniques which can be utilized to counter them effectively.

CHAPTER II

THE
CADRE PHASE
OF INSURGENCY

Despite tomes of evidence to the contrary, the birth of a Marxist or Communist insurgency is really very simple. First there must be an element in the population of a given country which has been impregnated with thoughts of revolution. Subsequent developments generally depend on the presence of two midwives:

- The Soviet Union concludes (or a surrogate power, such as Cuba, concludes) that the potential gains of clandestine intervention in a particular country exceed the risks.
- Intelligence officers are able to spot, assess, and recruit enough qualified candidates for political in-

doctrination and guerrilla warfare training to form a revolutionary nucleus, or cadre.

Having reached the conclusion that these conditions have been met, intelligence officers stationed in the country to be subverted intensify efforts to identify additional potential recruits. Directly, or through agents of the local Communist Party, they seek them out at cultural events, at trade union gatherings, at student meetings, and in all the eddies of society where the representatives of a foreign power are allowed to circulate. Not infrequently, while KGB officers or DGI operatives are trolling, they themselves are being sought by disaffected groups or individuals who, in the emotional state of revolt, have decided to solicit foreign funds, weapons, training, and guidance to pursue their own political aims violently.

Regardless of how and by whom the contact is initiated, the Communist officer and the potential insurgent eventually meet; in tradecraft terms, a recruitment target has thus been spotted. There ensues a feeling-out process during which the candidate is evaluated for intelligence, motivation, character, pyschological stability, leadership qualities, and charisma. How trainable is the target? Can he or she assume responsibility for training others? How will the target react in crisis? How much stress can the target bear? Will he or she be willing to rob, kidnap, knife, shoot, or blow up the innocent as well as the hated?

The Cadre Phase of Insurgency

If the evaluation is positive, the recruiting officer cultivates the target, not unlike a polished seducer. The seduction may be prolonged and subtle or relatively brief and direct. Ultimately the suitor must reveal his true intentions and ask the loaded question: Will you, or won't you? Is he or she willing to work for the revolution?

When such overtures are rejected, the fault usually can be traced to lust, a misjudgment of the target by the recruiter—and there is a seat waiting on the next plane to Moscow, reserved by either the embassy or the local government. Case histories show, however, that most recruitment offers are accepted if appraisal of the target has been made professionally and correctly. Recent Cuban successes in Nicaragua—in July 1979 insurgents maintaining extensive clandestine relations with Havana overthrew the government of President Anastasio Somoza—suggest that the Cubans and their Soviet tutors are today quite professional.

Upon recruitment the cadre candidate assumes a new life role, almost as the grub becomes an insect. It begins with his or her travel via a circuituous, secret route to the Soviet Union, Cuba, China, East Germany, or Czechoslovakia for basic training. A Peruvian traveling to the guerrilla warfare school of Cuba, for example, might fly first to Paris. There contact is made with an intelligence officer from the Cuban Embassy, who exchanges the recruit's passport for a Cuban travel document. This, plus an appropriate legend or cover story of who he is and why he is traveling, enables the cadre candidate to fly from Paris via Prague to Havana. The leaves in the Peruvian's bona fide passport do not reveal travel to Cuba. After three to six months' training the insurgent reverses his steps and returns to Paris, where he picks up his valid passport. He then returns to Peru, now one of the hard-core cadres charged with preparing the insurgency. Where has he been? At the Sorbonne, of course. And here are his grades, bills, and canceled checks to prove it—all, of course, clever forgeries.

The variations of tradecraft employed to transport candidates to training centers are limited only by the bounds of ingenuity. In Thailand, for example, in 1966 a potential cadre candidate was recruited in Bangkok by the Communist Party and shuttled overland by car, truck, bus, and train to the Thai-Lao border around Nongkhai, on the banks of the Mekong River. There he boarded a native boat. The swift current of the muddy Mekong soon carried the recruit to Vientiane, Laos, leaving, naturally, no tracks. At the open-air morning market the candidate next met with either a Chinese or a North Vietnamese official living in Vientiane. Tradecraft was scarcely a problem. A rich mixture of merchandise and people, the market was ideal for such clandestine meetings. It was Vientiane's crossroad at which Indian, Pakistani, Chinese, Thai, Lao, or Vietnamese merchants haggled with anyone who came to buy or look. Everyone was equal in the bumping, pushing, and shoving of the market, for amid the blending of body odors, dust, and burning sun, both the rich and the poor bought their food supplies for the day. Two more buyers made little difference. After a rendezvous next to a pre-determined vendor's stall, the recruit was on his way, by overland routes, to China or Vietnam for training.

What can we do at the earliest of all stages to inhibit the growth and development of the insurgency?

An insurgency is most likely to originate in an environment of harsh economic and social injustice, political repression, and pervasive corruption. Other factors, such as nationalism, a desire for regional autonomy or a rejection of standard values in a predominantly urban society, can also contribute to creating a climate for revolt. The resulting despair and frustration convince potential cadres that constructive change can come about only by a violent uprooting of the entire prevailing order. Meanwhile, others persuade foreign powers that assistance to the revolution may be profitable. There are always ears ready to listen.

Therefore, it would seem to be only a common-sense conclusion that one effective way of nipping an insurgency in the bud would be to encourage and assist threatened nations to undertake lasting social and economic reforms, thus to justify hopes of the population for a better future. Such a policy is simply enlightened self-interest. One technique successful in the past: local civic action programs which deny insurgents the allegiance of people in given areas.

Successful civic action programs have tried to meet the people's aspirations for improved educational, health or transportation facilities. When a government has come close to satisfying the needs of its constituency in a particular village or district, then guerrillas have been unable to flourish.

Even when shouldered with the best of will and skill, even when wisely and generously assisted from abroad, genuine progress in many third world countries is made at snail's pace. Political traditions and values have evolved over centuries in Western democracies. They cannot be instantly adopted in nations the roots of which are even more ancient. And even when accomplished, reform and progress will not necessarily prevent insurrection attempts. Nonetheless, they are better alternatives than plastic bombs.

Between World War II and 1970 few third world nations did more to better the lot of their citizenry than did Mexico. For example, the Mexican government reduced illiteracy from 85 to 17 percent, curbed disease among the rural population, raised per capita income almost fourfold. It built an infrastructure to exploit natural resources and more evenly to distribute their fruits. Although Mexico would hardly be considered a model of democracy by Western European or American standards, its people enjoyed incomparably greater freedoms than do Soviet citizens, including the right to criticize the monolithic ruling political party. Soviet citizens are not granted this modest privilege in their country.

Despite measurable progress, Mexico was far from safe. The KGB, through North Korean agents, recruited and trained a substantial insurgent cadre dedicated, in its words, to turning Mexico into "another Vietnam." Only a last-minute crackdown by Mexican authorities in March 1971 avoided widespread bloodshed.

The Federal Republic of Germany has built a model democracy which bestows political freedom and economic well-being upon its people. Their standards of living have nearly surpassed our own. Yet this did not abort the hatching of anti-establishment and anti-American terrorist cells such as the Baader-Meinhof gang, nor did it discourage the Soviet Union from attempting to assist them.

At the opposite end of the world, the island miracle of Japan spawned the Sekigun—the Japanese Red Army—which serves as hired guns for several of the most vicious terrorist gangs in existence, among them the Popular Front for the Liberation of Palestine (PFLP). Japan's healthy balance of payments, smoothly humming industries, and bountiful lifestyle helped isolate this group on the fringes of society. But it did not destroy the Sekigun, which remains waiting at anchor in such safe harbors as South Yemen and North Korea.

Who can say for sure what has bred them? A love-hate relationship with their fathers? A fury then turned against authority, mindless in its destructiveness? Whatever it is, no nation—even the United States—is immune from such aberrations. Take them for facts. They exist. Should they be tolerated and nurtured by the rational society they seek to destroy? And should we look on benignly as others assist them in this goal? If not, how should we deal with them?

From experience, we can see eight steps which, if taken in time, have been effective in combating an insurgency in its early, or cadre, phase. They seem, perhaps, overly obvious, childlike in simplicity. It is surprising how often they are ignored.

1. *Find out who is doing the recruiting.* The security and intelligence services of the menaced country bear primary responsibility for uncovering the identity of those enlisting or gang-pressing potential revolutionary operatives. They should be assisted by American experts to the extent that they need and ask for help in this mission.

One method consists of continuous surveillance of Communist embassies and personnel. By tracking their movements, analysts can establish a pattern and, in time, possibly the purpose of their activities. Deviations and contacts within the local population can betray recruiting efforts. Additionally, other insurgent contacts may be unearthed by photographing everyone entering and leaving an embassy, and then comparing the results with photos or "mug shots" of known or suspected terrorists.

Listening devices can yield a wealth of intelligence. Each embassy has a room regarded as secure; some are even lead-lined to foil electronic eavesdropping. Here intelligence officers discuss sensitive matters, such as efforts to initiate contacts with potential insurgents. If electronic devices can be introduced into these sanctuaries, extensive information about both the recruiters and who they are trying to recruit can be recorded.

2. *Learn how they are doing it and what procedures are being used in selecting cadre cadidates for training.* Experience has told us that each nation's intelligence forces often employ different—and sometimes specific—techniques of what we call tradecraft, or how one goes about the business of espionage. For example, Soviet master spy Rudolf Abel preferred hollow coins, bolts, shaving brushes, and batteries to hide and transmit messages. More recently, in Mexico City, Russian controllers ordered American satellite and code spies Christopher Boyce and Andrew Lee to communicate their desire for a meeting by placing a chalk mark on a light pole at a certain corner. It was a typical and often-used device. Notices in newspaper ad columns are also popular. Yet another KGB ploy: the "telephone tree," in which a contact is asked to be at a certain public phone booth at a specific address, on a specific day, at a specific time. If he is not there to receive a call from his control, he has been provided with the location of yet another booth, at a different address, a different time and day. And so on. These are called alternates—in case something goes wrong, one always can count on a prearranged alternative.

Much of this tradecraft is commonplace. And once recognized for what it is, the spoor is not at all difficult to follow. Unfortunately many of our friends in the so-called third world lack the experience and operational background to read the signs. If it is in our national interest to do so, we should provide them the advice and tools to protect themselves—as well as *ourselves*. Such expertise can include the techniques of installing telephone taps on embassy personnel, our own debriefings of Cuban and Soviet defectors, information acquired by our own agents in the enemy camp, stolen documents, and the interception of communications.

3. *Penetrate the spotting (who is the target?), assessment, and recruitment organization to identify the candidates selected for guerrilla warfare training.* An agent appropriately placed in the other camp's recruiting machinery can be better than a monkey wrench. The source cannot always identify cadre candidates by name, residence, and occupation. But often the penetration agent, if in the ranks of the hostile intelligence service, may have access to its support apparatus or the local Communist Party that can provide enough data concerning age, physical description, educational level, and family status information to allow the local security service, backed by worldwide United States resources, to identify the target candidate.

Once a positive identification has been made, legal action can be taken against the recruit at the appropriate time and place. It is important to note, however, that not all such potential terrorists or guerrillas should be arrested. There are advantages in tracking a cadre candidate until he leads the authorities to others in his cell or, for example, to arms caches.

Let us consider a hypothetical case. Suppose a penetration agent in the Chilean Communist Party reports in 1972 that he is scheduled to meet an unidentified male in Santiago to pass him funds for travel to Cuba. The hint is, of course, that a Chilean candidate is planning a clandestine trip. But subsequent events prove this false. The agent passes on the funds, as instructed, and obtains a good physical description of the contact, plus the distinct impression from a brief conversation that he is a Brazilian. With this as a starting point analysts can study airline passenger manifests from Chile, Brazil, and Mexico over a two-week period. Two prime suspects emerge. Each is eventually photographed, and the photographs are shown to the agent who has passed the funds. A positive identification of the Brazilian results. Monitoring of his activities leads to identification of other guerrilla candidates, thereby inhibiting the growth of an insurgency in Brazil. This is how it *should* happen, and although this example is not a summary of a real operation, it contains enough of the truth to make its point.

4. *Determine what to do about it or how selectively to disrupt by due process of law the cadre phase of insur-*

gency operations. Numerous options are available if there exists reliable information about what hostile intelligence services are doing to recruit cadre candidates. For example, the recruiting officer can suddenly be declared persona non grata by the country to which he is assigned. His expulsion can negate his recruitment accomplishments. If a KGB officer is forced to leave quickly for Moscow and his cadre candidates are still waiting to go abroad, an elaborate set of plans evaporates into thin air. Contact is broken between the candidates and the recruiter. A fallback position must be prepared, a replacement briefed and trained—all of which takes time. Meanwhile, the candidates themselves can be detained, denied passports, and prevented from leaving the country for training.

More sophisticated approaches can also be used if the host country has the manpower and skills to use them. For one, playing double-agent games can render the cadre candidate ineffective. The security service simply recruits the cadre candidate itself. It is true that this can be a dirty game. In the past it has involved blackmail, threats of a long prison sentence, and, in the case of our competition, the KGB, outright execution. Most profitably, however, the process of "turning" such a cadre candidate is no more painful than rational persuasion—a sane measure of what one stands to gain or to lose. In any event, nobody has ever claimed that the Marquiss of Queensberry invented plastic explosives.

5. *Don't hide it.* An aroused and well-informed citizenry is an effective deterrent to the type of spotting and assessment that has to take place if the Soviets and Cubans are to recruit cadre candidates. The people should be told what they can do to cripple insurgent activities. After all, it is *their* society which is at stake. Radio, television, and newspapers should be encouraged to launch a campaign exposing how foreign powers are attempting to recruit cadre candidates from among their audience. This can seriously impair recruitment efforts. And it is particularly effective if the campaign teaches how to help thwart enemy activities. For example, such an effort might be spearheaded by a television series on the KGB, dramatizing its mission and organization. Cases of Soviet espionage and efforts to incite revolution should be reconstructed. Biographic sketches might be provided on known KGB officers in the country concerned. The truth is rarely libelous. The concluding presentation would ask the people to report possible recruitment activities by the Soviets to an open telephone line manned by security or police officials around the clock.

6. *Find out how we can help, or how the United States can assist in the establishment and maintenance of an effective security agency in the target country.* The first line of defense in any counterinsurgency effort is an effective internal security service. This organization must be staffed with intelligent, dedicated, and incorruptible officers who have been trained

to use counterintelligence techniques to penetrate the cadre phase recruitment cycle. In most underdeveloped countries quality manpower is in short supply, and what little there is often seems to be snatched away by high-profile, more prestigious units, such as an air force. Given the sink-or-swim realities of internal disorder, leaders must put a greater percentage of talented young men in intelligence than they have in the past—and must pay them accordingly. It is no secret that corruption is rooted in poverty and inequality. In some third world nations—many of which are threatened by insurgencies today—judges are paid less than clerks, security forces less than either. The temptation is ever present to bribe and extort. It must be reduced. And parity in salary is one good place to start.

The security service should have arrest powers properly supervised by judicial review. What's more, it should have the modern capability to maintain computerized records on citizens traveling abroad.

Does this sound extreme? Not really—although such a step would be greeted by shrieks of paranoid hysteria in our own nation. Others find themselves quite able to accept such modest controls. Who they are might surprise you. Travelers in France—indeed, throughout most of Western Europe—are required to present their passports when booking into hotels. In Germany one carries an *Ausweis*, or identity card. And no one leaves England without first presenting proof to the government that he or she has paid up back taxes. The United States, naturally, is not threatened by an armed insurgency. But, then, neither are those European nations for the most part.

In order to undertake such practical measures, the service must earn the respect and confidence of its citizens. There can be no violation of the accepted norms of human rights, or the service becomes seriously disadvantaged.

Internally it must keep a clean house. Security standards within its own ranks must be rigorous enough so that our intelligence officers—together with other foreign liaison services—can feel comfortable when they exchange sensitive data. There must be minimal risk that such information will be compromised by indiscretion, corruption, or treason. Call it, for want of a better word, *trust*.

Israel's Shin Beth, which is responsible for internal security, is a first class agency. It is the primary reason why the PLO has had only limited success operating in either Galilee through Israeli Arabs or on the West Bank through its indigenous Arab agents who are PLO adherents. Frustrated Palestinian terrorists now resort to other tactics to attack targets in Israel. One such tactic is the launching of commando teams at sea in small rubber rafts, but this is difficult because of heavy seas, navigation and maneuvering problems, and the risks of detection by heavily armed Israeli patrols at sea or on land. These obstacles have frustrated most seaborne attempts by Palestinians to penetrate Israeli defenses.

Other attempts—most by infiltration from Lebanon and Jordan—have also proved hazardous. Often terrorist teams are intercepted by security forces at their crossing point, for word of their arrival has preceded them. When such groups do manage to penetrate the frontier undetected, their targets are frequently indiscriminate and strictly those of opportunity—such as innocent women and children. This countering of the Palestinian threat by Shin Beth and its sister service, Mossad, which handles foreign intelligence, is a textbook example of how a third world nation should fashion its own secret services. And, frankly, it does as good a job of advising other third world countries on this topic as does the United States. In sum, an effective security agency is a country's first line of defense because it narrows or closes potential avenues of attack by enemies—diverts their efforts onto side streets where they can better be contained.

7. *Guide governments in the preparation of antiterrorist laws.* When the cadre phase begins to unfold, many countries find they do not have laws on the books to deal with the threat. It is critical that a government be able to neutralize Soviet- or Cuban-supported revolutionaries, not by sending them into exile but by putting them in jail. The basis for confinement is particularly important. Put another way, it is better to be able to arrest and convict subversives on the basis of a *law* than on an executive *order*. If such laws cannot be passed expeditiously, the party in power should

mount an education campaign to rally public opinion in behalf of their enactment.

8. *Assist the host country's military or police forces to establish and train an elite antiguerrilla unit.* Once the cadre phase has begun, a country must accept that it may not be able to prevent the insurgency from advancing to the next and more dangerous stage. To prepare for this development, the friendly government should organize a special antiguerrilla unit, staffed by elite military or police personnel. The strength of the unit should derive from quality of personnel, their training and leadership, from mobility, firepower, communications, and tactics, rather than from numbers. Initially the size of the unit need not exceed one 550-man battalion.

This elite strike force should be formed as soon as the cadre phase of insurgency has been detected. Later there will be scarce time to build it when the guerrillas' "war of national liberation" actually begins in earnest. Experience in Vietnam and elsewhere has shown that the selection and training of personnel who will conduct combat operations should be completed at least sixteen weeks before there is an actual need to use them in the field. Emphasis in training should focus on the unit's ability to move and attack with lightning speed—and without telegraphing the knock-out punch.

A drama that unfolded in Bolivia in 1967 offers an example of how this tactic can pay off. The Bolivian government requested counterinsurgency assistance from the United States after learning that Che Guevara—alias Ramón Benítez—had established a guerrilla base in the mountainous area in the southeastern part of the country. The United States sent a mobile Special Forces training team from Fort Gulick in the Canal Zone to Bolivia to train a Bolivian ranger battalion in counterinsurgency techniques. Training was still in progress when local Bolivian forces in the area received intelligence that Che and his small band had been spotted nearby. American advisers recommended airlifting the special Bolivian battalion now nearing completion of its training to the area, and on October 1, 1967, it was deployed in a rugged, heavily jungled area called the Valle Grande.

Six days after the unit took to the field, informants reported the presence of a band of suspicious strangers—some armed—in a village not far away. The battalion immediately picked up their trail. It took them a week to corner the group. On October 8 they engaged in a fire fight with Che's band, which, cornered and outgunned, was soon destroyed. Survivors fled. The next day Che himself was captured.

Much nonsense has been written about the circumstances surrounding Che's death. The fact is that Che was executed because of widespread charges of Bolivian ineptitude in dealing with Che's guerrillas.

One particularly galling source of this ridicule had been Régis Debray—French Marxist and Che's confidant—who had interviewed Guevara in his Bolivian hideout in March 1967. As a result, Debray was arrested by Bolivian authorities. During his highly publicized trial, Che's admirer taunted Bolivia's security forces as being inept, incompetent, worse than Keystone Kops. This humiliation sealed Che's death warrant. To erase this popular impression, Che was taken from his detention area and summarily shot by a one-man firing squad at a secret location in the countryside—without, I might stress, the knowledge of any U.S. agency or representative.

A postmortem on the destruction of Che's guerrilla cadres clearly shows that in this case the United States responded promptly and properly to a friendly nation's plea for help. The Bolivians used the aid intelligently and effectively. The results derailed Castro's export of the revolution to Latin America for more than a decade. Several Latin nations were able to use this breathing spell to attack the social and economic ills that breed and sustain similar insurgent movements.

The lesson: When governments friendly to the United States are threatened by Communist-initiated or -sponsored insurgencies—but lack the experience to cope with the problem—the United States must consider if it is in its interest to provide the third option. The go or no-go decision should be approached with realism, not timidity. The third option can provide solutions that other, longer-range programs of reform and economic aid cannot resolve until the violence ends.

Our decision to help must always be a *political* decision, made by legally constituted *civilian* authorities who bear responsibility for the conduct of our foreign policy. But it is the duty of the U.S. intelligence community, particularly those with covert action experience and responsibility, to forewarn policy makers of the birth of such an insurgency, to assess the risks of acting and of not acting, to explain just what the third option will entail.

Similarly it is the duty of the Defense Department, which is legally responsible for military security of the nation, to add its own assessments. But in a democracy the final decision must rest with the chosen representatives of the electorate.

In deciding whether to invoke the third option, policy makers must frequently deal with the argument that we should not help a particular nation defend itself because its government is not democratic. This argument should be considered in the context of world realities. For example, of the 152 sovereign states belonging to the United Nations, only 33 can be classified as democratic by the most generous and elastic of definitions. If we adopt the position that we will help only those societies which presently meet our own democratic standards (which we ourselves do not always perfectly apply), then we isolate ourselves from the majority of mankind and forfeit much of our power to control global events. Worst of all, we abandon the majority of nations—

allies and neutrals alike—to the whims of our adversaries, who have repeatedly demonstrated their intention to impose their will on others. Encouraging such a scenario is not only dangerous but ludicrous and irresponsible. We are fooling no one but ourselves.

Policy makers must appreciate that the mere existence of many modern-day insurgencies does not per se mean that they are always justified or that their success will liberate and enrich the lives of the population affected. Can any serious, informed student—whatever his political persuasion—honestly contend that the people of Iran today are better off than they were before the 1979 revolution in Iran? Can anyone argue that the tortured, starved, massacred people of Cambodia have profited by the success of Hanoi's "war of national liberation" in Southeast Asia—or from their own Khmer Rouge insurgents?

Let us not be hypocrites. At the bottom of all this lies our own self-interest. Was, for example, the Marshall Plan a good-guy gift to a war-torn Europe? It wasn't. Its implementation was the result of cold reality. Did we or did we not want a weakened Western Europe—easy prey for Stalin's Soviet Union bent on expanding its influence by whatever means appropriate? The Marshall Plan not only thwarted the Kremlin's intentions in such nations as Greece and West Germany but served our own security by rebuilding and toughening former allies and enemies. It is not by accident that West Germany—now thoroughly democratized—is America's most powerful ally. Was this immoral? Only a Mad Hatter would say yes.

The same principles apply to the third option.

CHAPTER III

THE
SPANISH BASQUES
—A Case Study of
the Cadre Phase

The Spanish Basque movement merits study because it illustrates many characteristics of a budding insurgency which, for all its destructiveness, has been unable to advance beyond the cadre phase. The recent history of the movement also shows how timely political action can inhibit and contain such a movement.

Ever since 1937, when General Francisco Franco abolished the autonomous government of the Basque region, many Basques—a hardy mountain folk of northern Spain—have longed for restoration of autonomy or outright independence. After World War II more moderate nationalists hoped the United States would help in reward for Basque assistance to

French and Italian underground cells in the fight against Germany. In 1953 these expectations evaporated after the United States negotiated an agreement for military and naval bases in Spain with Franco, a staunch enemy of Basque independence. Even the most temperate leaders, such as José Antonio de Aguirre, who headed the Basque government in exile, recognized that on the cold war scale of values, the United States ranked the goodwill of the Spanish state far above that of a nationalistic minority consisting of only some 2.5 million people.

In 1958 frustrations spawned a covert independence movement, Basque Homeland and Liberty (ETA), which advocated a separate nation consisting of the four Basque provinces in Spain and the three in France. Naturally this was unacceptable to either Paris or Madrid. ETA was based—as many such movements are—on a dual structure: a political branch and a military branch, the ETA/M—or action/military service—staffed and run by cadres dedicated to attainment of political ends through violence and terror. The ETA/M is highly disciplined, difficult to penetrate, because most members have known each other since childhood. Being familiar with each other's behavior and patterns of life, they are quick to detect collaboration with the authorities. Treason is swiftly dealt with by execution. The terrorist cadres have the advantage of operating on their own turf, so to speak, familiar terrain where they know every nook and cranny. Pressed, they are able to flee government pursuit by escaping across the border into safe houses among France's Basque community in cities like Bayonne and nearby Biarritz.

There is evidence that KGB and ETA/M representatives have met in Paris as well as in Spain. Indeed, the Basque separatists make up only several threads of an intricate web of terrorist connections which spans the world, and the role of the splicer is often played by Soviet or Cuban agents. For example, the ETA also maintains ties in France with the Revolutionary Coordinating Junta (JCR), a grouping of Latin American terrorist organizations, which in turn enjoys give-and-take with Cuban "sympathizers." How do they use one another and for what? From available information it appears that arms, including assault rifles, rockets, submachine guns, and grenades, are smuggled to Paris in Cuban or Libyan diplomatic pouches—a favorite ploy. The weapons are then funneled through Basque channels in France into ETA/M's hands in Spain. Bulkier explosives have been obtained by raids on government installations and construction sites. Basque terrorists have acquired some money through bank robberies—"expropriations," they are called—and have accepted foreign funding from Libya, which has bankrolled movements from Belfast to Mindanao in the Philippines. Meanwhile, small numbers of ETA/M terrorists have undergone guerrilla warfare training in Algeria. A handful may have gained actual combat experience since 1977 by fighting with the Algerian-sponsored Polisario Front in the Western Sahara.

On December 20, 1973, Basque terrorists assassinated Prime Minister Luis Carrero Blanco, heir apparent to Generalissimo Franco. This proved to be one of those terrorist acts which had profound effects unforeseen by the assassins. Blanco's death enabled King Juan Carlos to assume the leadership of Spain after the death of Franco in 1975. Though young and inexperienced, Juan Carlos saw the need to channel Spanish society back to democracy. In one of his wisest actions, he selected as prime minister Adolfo Suárez, a strong, sensitive, and visionary politician.

Although sorely provoked by continuing killings and bombings, the Spanish leaders resisted pressure from the military to retaliate with repression. Instead, they sought to gratify the desires of Basques for more control of their own affairs without jeopardizing the glue which bound Spain into a single nation. But in so doing, they had to consider and contend with three different political parties in the Basque region, each of which felt itself entitled to a greater role in self-government than the others.

The largest, the Basque National Party (PNV), while willing to consult with the government about effecting peaceful change in the status of the Basque region, nevertheless winked approvingly at ETA/M activities, considering them a useful prod to Madrid. Next, the Spanish Socialist Workers Party (PSOE), displayed even less willingness to cooperate with the central government in curbing terrorism. And a third party, Herri Batasuna (People's Unity)—it could claim only 10 percent of Basque votes—openly supported the ETA. Given this mixture of power,

The Spanish Basques

the government could field no organized or local political opponent against the ETA. Thus, the task of suppressing terrorism in the Basque region, as well as defending against its spread, fell solely upon the Spanish police and military.

In 1979, however, Suárez maneuvered to change the political equation and isolate the ETA from the Basque political mainstream. Sensing the danger, the ETA/M launched a new wave of terror aimed at disrupting negotiations between the government and the Basque National Party. On January 3, 1979, its gunmen shot the military governor of Madrid, General Constantino Ortín Gil, and on May 25 they assassinated General Luis Gómez Hortigüela in Madrid, killing in the meantime a number of lesser military and police officials.

Despite these provocations, the government persisted in its search for a peaceful solution to Basque autonomy, and on July 17, 1979, it finally succeeded in negotiating a home rule agreement, the Guernica Statute, which called for elections to establish an autonomous Basque government. Again, the ETA/M reacted violently. On July 28 it attacked police patrols in Bilbao and San Sebastián, killing three officers and wounding four. The next day bombs exploded in each of Madrid's two main railway stations and at the airport, killing four civilians and wounding at least 113. The ETA/M quickly claimed credit for the carnage. No one doubted the claim.

Nevertheless, Suárez and the Basque National Party continued to negotiate. In August they agreed upon a far-reaching statute to the home rule agreement which provided that control of the police, education, broadcasting, and some taxation would be gradually transferred to the new regional government.

The ETA immediately recognized the dangers. The statute and the referendum scheduled for October 25, 1979, would eliminate much of the restiveness in the Basque region, thus its own need to exist. The ETA/M ordered Herri Batasuna, its overt political party, to urge voters to abstain from the referendum. It argued the statute did not recognize the right of the Basque people to self-determination. In contrast, the Basque National Party, which played such a critical role in making a referendum possible, marshaled all its resources to get out the vote. The Catholic Church—a powerful force in its own right—also made clear that it favored the autonomy statute.

Again, the ETA reacted ferociously. This time, on September 23, 1979, gunmen murdered the military general of San Sebastián Province, Lieutenant General Lorenzo González Valles y Sánchez. On October 8, 1979, terrorists in San Sebastián sprayed a bar frequented by police personnel with submachine gunfire, wounding eleven people. The same day a police inspector was killed in the Basque city of Pamplona, and terrorists killed two noncommissioned officers of the paramilitary Civil Guard in Santander. These murders raised the number of political killings committed in Spain to that date to 114.

The Spanish Basques

About 1.5 million Basques, eighteen or older, were eligible to vote in the October referendum and 60 percent of them cast ballots. The results were an overwhelming endorsement of the agreements restoring autonomous government. The actual election took place in March 1980, and the moderate Basque National Party received a twenty-five-seat mandate to form the new regional government.

Today the hard-core cadre of the ETA/M has shrunk to no more than 200 men. Their immediate prospects for recruiting more manpower among Basques, many of whom have recoiled from the past terrorism and are concerned with building the future, are not promising. Because of the patience and persistence of Suárez, the ETA/M will now be confronted by Basque, as well as Spanish, police and military authorities. More than anyone else, they have a vested interest in preserving law and order in the region.

Still, the Spanish military remains concerned about instability in the Basque area, where last year 80,000 of a one-million labor force were unemployed. Some fear that the Basques will be only temporarily satisfied with local autonomy, that soon they will plot to exploit it as a foundation for total independence. To prevent this, the military is prepared to intervene with massive force, if necessary. Nothing would more delight the ETA. It would discredit moderates in the Basque National Party and revive ETA chances of rallying the people. We told you so, they will crow.

This desire to provoke heavy-handed intervention or repression has resulted in ETA commanders' singling out important military personnel for assassination. Prime Minister Suárez, while politically sensitive to the concerns of the military, is nonetheless unlikely to adopt extreme measures in the Basque region unless they are unavoidable. He understands that such political insensitivity could ignite an escalating chain reaction of violence and repression that would destroy progress so far and drive a permanent stake into the heart of Spain's modern experiment with democracy. Yet every attack upon an army officer or a Spanish civilian makes it that much more difficult for the Spanish government to do anything which smacks of appeasing terrorism. Thus, although the Basque insurgency has been contained in its puberty phase, it still poses a danger. Spanish interests and those of all nations, including the United States—let us not forget our nuclear submarine base at Rota as well as Spain's desire to join NATO—demand that Basque terrorism be kept off-balance.

Spain has the capability to deal with the insurgents on a military basis. Its leaders have also demonstrated that they can cope on a political level. It remains for them to enlist the support of elected Basque authorities to apply jointly the basic counterinsurgency steps that have proved so effective against the cadre stage and once and for all eliminate the cancer, not with a sledgehammer, but with a scalpel. Otherwise, the patient will not survive the operation.

But Spain also needs and deserves assistance from its friends.

France, for one, could help by assigning more police and intelligence resources to deny Basque terrorists sanctuaries into which they periodically retreat along the French/Spanish border areas. France also might do more to intensify surveillance and penetration of Soviet, Cuban, and Libyan intelligence establishments based out of Paris. The Revolutionary Coordinating Junta should also become a prime target, thus unmasking and interdicting foreign support of the ETA. This, then, is in France's interests.

As for the United States, it could help such a joint French-Spanish effort by providing intelligence gathered by our worldwide networks. Frequently we have access to sources which are denied to either the French or the Spanish secret services. For example, we may acquire an "asset" who has penetrated the Puerto Rican terrorist movement in its European activities and can supply intelligence of Basque links to Cuban operatives—or a forthcoming arms deal. Would it shock you to learn that we discovered not long ago that a certain "Middle East" nation was planning to transship arms via the United States— hidden in the household effects of one of its diplomats? The cargo: hand-held antiaircraft missiles. Who is to say what their destination was—perhaps a rooming house in Queens from which they could be fired at, for example, a low-flying passenger jet from Kennedy International Airport. The name on the fuselage is inconsequential. But it could easily have been Iberian Airlines. Such is the nature of the enemy. The United States could help Spain cope with this threat by assigning two professional intelligence officers to work with Madrid on this specific insurgency problem. The two officers would require about $100,000 in annual expenditures to support joint operations which would be targeted on Basque agents who could furnish the intelligence needed to prevent major terrorist-inspired disasters from occurring. This parsimonious investment could nonetheless buy much—not the least of which is some peace of mind for ourselves and our allies.

CHAPTER IV

THE
INCIPIENT PHASE

An insurgency enters what we call the incipient phase once cadres have been trained and begin building the subterranean infrastructure required to mount sustained operations rather than acts of terrorism. To lay this hidden foundation, the cadres establish bases within defined operational areas. Arms, ammunition, and explosives must be purchased or otherwise acquired from foreign supporters, then cached. Meanwhile, channels for resupply of both material and recruits must be opened, broadened, and protected.

Most important, the revolution must attract ever-increasing manpower—for this is the lifeblood of prolonged struggle. Without it, combat losses cannot be replaced; cadre cells—the core of it all—cannot be rebuilt if exposed and shattered by security forces. One devastating example: the Viet Cong's ill-timed Tet offensive in 1968. While American TV viewers convinced themselves that North Vietnamese and Viet Cong forces had scored a resounding victory, the facts clearly showed otherwise. For the insurgents, Tet was a Waterloo. Thousands surfaced in expectation of a quick defeat of U.S. and Saigon troops. One by one, they were killed or captured. The cream of the Viet Cong's cadres were lost—and only direct North Vietnamese intervention ultimately worked.

If effective, political indoctrination and guerrilla warfare instruction abroad have equipped returning cadres with an intimate and working knowledge of how to use the basic tools of terrorism and revolution. They are familiar with firearms and explosives, as well as other—even nastier—instruments of torture and death. They know how to compartmentalize insurgent teams so that one does not know of the existence of the next—thus cannot betray it. They have learned countersurveillance to prevent disastrous penetration. They have learned how to conceal and support themselves in either the rural or the urban environment where they are to function; swim as a fish in the sea, Mao called it. They have at least rudimentary knowledge of clandestine communications.

Ideally, in any case from the standpoint of their foreign sponsors, they have pledged themselves to a fanatical, revolutionary morality that justifies slaughter of the innocent and destruction of society, and they have a zeal that enables them to pass on the germ of insurgency like so many Typhoid Marys. It matters little whether the slogans bear no relation to reality. What is important is that *they* believe. And they are able to make others believe.

Typically, cadres slip back into their homeland in small groups at different times and by various routes. Some, most reliable, will have been provided with avenues through which they can communicate with their often-impatient sponsors. Frequently used channels include agents within the local Communist Party or, in some noteworthy cases, intelligence officers working out of Soviet, Cuban, or East European embassies. Sometimes clandestine meetings are arranged in a neighboring country where they are less conspicuous.

Customarily cadres divide into cells or groups of no more than five to ten people. The first critical task for a cadre is to neutralize the area in which it has chosen to operate, then to develop a sanctuary in the form of a "safe house" or camp. The selection must be made wisely. A misjudgment of location, the attitudes of its inhabitants, and terrain can be fatal.

A rural operational base camp must be carefully scouted. What about concealment and water? Is there enough? There should also be several different ways by which guerrillas can enter or flee. Once established, the guerrillas must cultivate the goodwill of peasants in the surrounding area, usually within a radius of a six-hour march—enough warning time of approaching security forces to allow insurgents to flee. From villagers close by the guerrillas can acquire an intimate knowledge of terrain, local trails, water holes, and hiding places that will permit them to survive. In time, and if won over, peasants may offer such logistical support as food and medicine or volunteers as porters—to say nothing of serving as the insurgents' eyes and ears. And peasants will be a source of indispensable intelligence when the cadre is planning operations or is evading or ambushing government forces.

Once they have mastered their new environment and gain confidence that they can survive and prosper in it, the guerrillas organize civic action programs, such as assisting the local residents to dig wells or repair their homes. But nothing comes free. Along with this assistance local villagers can expect a steady diet of political indoctrination. This widens the guerrillas' support horizons as the audience increases. But it inevitably brings them into conflict with those who object and will not be bamboozled by sheer rhetoric. Like a spectator at a bad circus act, they are apt to throw eggs at the carnival barker. The insurgents soon turn to assassinating and burning the property of such cynics.

This, in turn, tends to polarize political views in the operational area. There is muscle behind the talk, after all. As the terrorizing of doubting Thomases intensifies, so do the bonds of commitment by supporters. Gradually the band gains new recruits. They may have grievances against the government, or they may simply seek adventure. Whatever their reasons, they are by now convinced that these insurgents in their midst mean business. The band cleverly exploits these diverse motivations, and as new recruits are enrolled, they are trained and equipped. By addition of local recruits, the band gains more tactical flexibility. Many can farm by day and play guerrilla by night. The insurgency begins to emerge from the incipient phase once the cadre cells have consolidated their bases, cached arms and supplies, and significantly increased their numbers through local recruiting. When the band successfully employs force against government installations and survives the initial retaliatory measures of police or conventional military forces, it is finally free of its incipient stage cocoon.

There are specific actions security forces can take to prevent this newest of insurgency metamorphoses. Let's examine a few of them. They are:

1. *Identify the guerrilla cadres as they reenter the country or quickly thereafter.* If security services unmasked a trainee scheduled to go abroad during the first, or cadre, phase but failed to prevent the journey, an efficient travel monitoring system still may spot the subject when he or she returns. Penetrations of the local Communist Party can result in advance word of travel plans. Intensive surveillance of the Soviet, Chinese, or Cuban embassies, using previ-

ously described techniques, may also lead watchers to newly returned cadres.

If ever an objective and authoritative history of American counterinsurgency operations in Vietnam sees the light of day, it surely will reveal that we made many mistakes. However, it will also reveal tactics that were used successfully. Much of our experience in counterinsurgency was gained through the prolonged involvement in Vietnam. We must heed its lessons. It would be folly to fail to profit from our errors. But it would be stupid to ignore and fail to apply methods which proved effective.

We found the Viet Cong apparatus to be highly compartmented. Penetration was therefore difficult. Meanwhile, however, we had found that many Viet Cong cadres, using multiple aliases, were training at base areas in neighboring Cambodia. Members of the Viet Cong Saigon City Committee traveled to and from these camps with the regularity of homing pigeons. This predictabilty was a weakness which cadre leaders had overlooked. But we had not. To exploit it, American advisers developed the concept of what we called—for lack of something better—*Dai Phong* or "Big Wind." It was implemented by our Vietnamese counterparts in the Special Police. Essentially the plan was based on the exploitation of Viet Cong prisoners. For example, if a detained member of the Saigon City Committee revealed under questioning that he had been trained at one of three Cambodian sanctuaries, he would be asked to describe his fellow students and instructors.

Frequently Viet Cong cadres not previously known to the Special Police were thus identified. But the question then arose: What to do about it? Under the *Dai Phong* plan cooperative Viet Cong cadre members were disguised in police uniforms and stationed at a key checkpoint where all people and vehicles entering Saigon were either searched or their travel documents examined. It was a slow and often fruitless task. But we kept at it. A former cadre member might be in place at a checkpoint for weeks. Despite the boredom and frustration, the plan ultimately paid off when a Viet Cong, trying to infiltrate back into Saigon from Cambodia, was recognized by his former comrade. Now began the ticklish part. When such an identification was made, the informant signaled his controller with "body language"—a slight wave of a hand, a smile, or whatever had been agreed on. The police would then begin surveillance of the suspect, which they would maintain day and night until he led them to other Viet Cong cadres.

At this point a decision would be made whether or not to make wholesale arrests or to continue monitoring the cadres in hopes they would lead further up the Viet Cong chain of command. This approach was singularly successful in reducing Communist cadre activities and attacks in the Saigon area from 1969 to 1972.

2. *Locate the urban and rural safe houses that the cadres have established to support the incipient phase of guerrilla operations.* At first glance this seems like finding a needle in the haystack. Actually, no magic is required—if the security service is moderately competent in counterintelligence techniques. Safe houses can be located through surveillance of the identified trainee once he has returned home. Additionally, safe houses can be uncovered by recruited agents from among local Communist Party functionaries or, if one is very, very lucky, in the local *residenturas*[6] of the Soviet, Chinese, or Cuban intelligence services. Another productive source can be rural and urban informants whom the local service has seeded in enemy operational areas. Residents can detect changes in a community's living patterns much the way a doctor can determine an increase in pulsebeat. New or suspicious tenants are noted instantly. An unexplained transfer of property becomes a subject of gossip—all should be tapped. Agents locally "in place" are in a position to hear even the grass grow. Their contributions are pearls of intelligence.

Rural informant programs have been used as effective counterinsurgency tools in Malaysia and the Philippines as well as in South Vietnam, where in 1970 the Special Police maintained more than 5,000 sources on the payroll. These eyes and ears of the security service regularly provided a

[6]The field unit of a Communist intelligence service operating under diplomatic or commercial cover from offices in an embassy.

mass of reports that required painstaking analysis and sorting at district or province level. If accurate, analysis produced hard intelligence about where Viet Cong cadres were meeting with fellow conspirators. Monitoring of these meetings through electronic devices or informants disclosed the plans, intentions, and capabilities of Viet Cong organizations at the district and province level. Armed with this intelligence, the police or the South Vietnamese military could counter attacks or ambushes before they even got under way.

3. *Identify and disrupt channels for arms and ammunition.* In most countries the government requires citizens to obtain permits to own or buy firearms; thus, the acquisition of five to ten weapons is a major project for a guerrilla armorer. Generally speaking, weapons must be smuggled into the country by covert channels run by the local Communist Party. The diplomatic pouch of a foreign supporter like the Cuban DGI is one popular ruse. But if aware of the dangers, customs, border patrols, police, and military forces can often throttle the supply of weapons. Obviously interdiction of arms supplies can be like shooting ducks in a bathtub if—and this is a big, capital "if"—your own agents can be inserted into the smuggling chain, the Communist Party, or the hostile intelligence *residentura.*

4. *Gain intimate knowledge of terrain which appears best suited for a guerrilla base.* Analysis by maps, aerial photography, and information from local au-

thorities can pinpoint potential base camp locations. Where, for example, are the water holes, rivers, and clearings, and how about main trails? What about potential ambush locations? These all can be triangulated and then pinpointed, predicated on the assumption that guerrillas generally operate a reasonable day's march from a base site. In short, you may now know what an enemy will do and how he will go about it—even before he does. Once that is done, drop zones or helicopter landing areas should be marked for later use by the government's elite antiguerrilla unit. So you have managed to prepare the battleground to your liking, not the guerrillas'.

5. *Establish informant networks in potential guerrilla operational areas.* Don't wait for the enemy's arrival. Have selected informants planted in villages throughout the chosen area. The number of informants required depends on such diverse factors as terrain, population density, type of agriculture that is practiced in the area, and means of transportation in and out of the district. The broader the society, the more varied its life-style, the greater the number of "in place assets" needed. A network of this type can be controlled and serviced by local police units. The key to its very existence: to provide advance word that a guerrilla band has moved into the area. Once that fact is established—plus what security forces have already gleaned about the area—the network can provide the tactical intelligence needed to make the government's antiguerrilla unit combat-effective.

The Incipient Phase

6. *Organize effective civic action programs to encourage and reward loyalty to the government among the local population.* Civic action can be important if it delivers what it promises. It can convince the people that steps are really being taken to improve their lives. Programs should be designed to attack social, economic, and political evils. Corrupt, repressive, and incompetent local officials *must* be removed. Next comes the improvement of the local economy: the digging of water wells, the building of bridges and hospital dispensaries. Schools must be opened and professionally staffed. New agricultural techniques can be taught, and harvests increased tenfold through the use of seed stock programs.

A full range of American-sponsored civic action programs functioned in Laos during the 1961–1973 period. They had had two goals. The first was to improve the quality of life among the hill tribes of North Laos so that they might see that the royal Lao government was interested in their economic and social well-being as well as in their fighting qualities. During my service in Laos we developed fishponds, established pig breeding centers, and managed vocational schools which taught carpentry, brickmaking, and auto mechanics.

Our civic action effort opened cooperative retail stores to break the monopoly of Chinese merchants over manufactured goods that had been sold in hill tribe villages at exorbitant prices. This project was particularly well received by the Meo, for it convinced them of our concern for their economic needs. The Meo were quick to recognize that one does not eat rhetoric and propaganda. At best, the leaflets can fuel campfires in cold weather.

The second goal was the development of a sense of national identity among the hill tribes so that the concept of a Lao nation could in time be accepted by a society that had been traditionally nomadic. The teaching of a common Lao tongue rather than tribal dialect became an important part of the school curriculum. Meanwhile, newly opened hospitals, clinics, and dispensaries brought tribes together through the common need for health care. Supported by the central government, all this contributed to developing a sense of national identity.

The nation-building process was assisted by use of radio to transmit basic messages to the hill tribes, supplying practical information on crop developments while simultaneously undertaking political education to build morale, a sense of national identity, and patriotism.

In Laos, at least, civic action produced results. It won and kept the "hearts and minds" of the majority of the hill tribes on the side of the royal Lao government for more than twelve years.

7. *Initiate antiguerrilla operations with the elite unit as soon as tactical intelligence reveals the presence of a guerrilla band.* Nothing is so effective in stopping the development of an insurgency as the neutralization of those who, having finished training in

the Soviet Union, China, or Cuba, have taken to the field for the first time. Pressure, increasing pressure, must be applied: raids on guerrilla base camps, ambushes, sustained pursuit, and the denial of water and supplies. Pressure. Pressure. Pressure. Often the guerrillas—weakened by constant pursuit and harassment—will turn and fight. When they are thus brought to bay, the government must concentrate all the firepower necessary to destroy them if they choose not to surrender. The scalpel may now be discarded; the sledgehammer, swung.

The Provincial Reconnaissance Unit (PRU), organized by the South Vietnamese with American help into an elite anti-Viet Cong force, provides a classic case in point. Its mission was to collect intelligence on the Viet Cong Infrastructure (VCI) and use this to take the war to the armed insurgents. The PRU was deployed to all provinces. Generally, each unit consisted of no more than 100 men.

These units were at various times under the control of the province chief or, in the later stages of the war, the senior province police official. Sources for quality intelligence ranged from Phung Hoang (Phoenix) intelligence and operations centers to informants to captured documents. With such solid intelligence on file the PRU could plan, for example, a surgical operation designed to capture or eliminate a particular Viet Cong cell. Such missions were always approved in advance by the Vietnamese province chief or his deputy. Once sanctioned, the attack was carried out with the suddenness of a thunderclap. Delays risked security leaks.

The PRU operated largely at night and managed to score spectacular successes. Although its tactics often thrust it into costly fire fights with the Viet Cong, the ratio over any month was always highly favorable to the PRU. Its units were well trained and highly motivated. They exploited the element of surprise to the fullest and operated on the basis of sound intelligence. In the first six months of 1971 the PRU averaged more than 500 VCI captured per month throughout South Vietnam and about 120 killed. In contrast, the PRU suffered about 60 wounded per month, 10 killed. Most significant, this extremely effective combat ratio was achieved within the *legal* framework of the South Vietnamese system that existed during a period of war.

The PRU impact was not lost on the enemy. Debriefings of captured VCI frequently elicited statements that they feared the PRU more than any other South Vietnamese unit because it consistently hit the VCI in its base area. The testimony of one's enemy is frequently the most eloquent evidence of success.

The preceding techniques must be used simultaneously, not piecemeal, to attack the incipient phase of an insurgency. They are cost-effective, bureau-

The Incipient Phase

cratic inspectors might say, because they can save a significant loss of life in later phases of an insurgency—not to mention the independence of a sovereign state.

CHAPTER V

EL SALVADOR
—A Case Study
of the Incipient Phase

In July 1979 the Sandinista victory in Nicaragua sent political shock waves through Latin America. Despite what many Americans believed, the defeat and ouster of President Anastasio Somoza was viewed by both conservatives and liberals in many Latin American nations as proof of the decline of United States power and prestige. Whatever your political preference, the fact is that by not intervening decisively, either overtly or covertly, to bring about a more orderly transition of power in Nicaragua, we showed conclusively that we had no stomach to protect what Latin Americans see as important U.S. interests in Central America. Our impotence confused the left, frightened the right, and bred a new unstable political climate in Central America.

But the impact was not felt in Latin America alone. Signals were received in faraway places. In the Middle East the PLO—always to be counted on as an ally in such "wars of liberation"—threw its support behind the Sandinistas in return for recognition once the struggle was won. Operating from their base in Kingston, Jamaica, they actually sent Fedayeen advisers to assist the guerrillas, as well as trained Sandinista cadres in Palestinian camps. From around the world, terrorist organizations and Communist supporters alike arrived like hyenas to feed on the carcass.

Cuba, never one to look a gift horse in the mouth, took appropriate note of this new reality. Fidel Castro quickly reshaped his concepts of how to export revolution to Central America and the Caribbean in the 1980s. Previously Havana had paid more attention to Nicaragua, Guatemala, and Honduras than to El Salvador. Having been satisfied with inches, he now took yards. During 1979 the insurgency in El Salvador rocketed from the cadre to the incipient phase. By February that year approximately fifty members of the urban terrorist organization Farabundo Martí Popular Liberation Forces (FPL) slipped into Cuba for guerrilla warfare training. Upon completion of this course, they returned home to form the core and leadership of a "Popular Militia" force under the FPL.

The FPL's namesake—Farabundo Martí—was a Communist killed by security forces in a 1932 peasant revolt. But the FPL itself, an offshoot of the Salvador Revolutionary Action Party, was not born until 1972. Its founder and leader, Salvador Cayetano Carpio, was a former secretary-general of the Communist Party of El Salvador (PCES). But because the party rejected terrorism, he broke from it and struck out on his own. Under his firebrand leadership the FPL trumpets a revolutionary Marxist creed. Hardly news, its villains are "foreign imperialists"; its goals, the overthrow of existing order and the establishment of a Communist society.

By 1976 the FPL was bombing such targets as the offices of the National Conciliation Party (PCN), National Guard posts, and commercial properties. For funds it kidnapped people for ransom. Alarmed, the El Salvador government hit back and succeeded in rounding up key cadres. The FPL went to ground to lick its wounds, which, while serious, were not fatal. It concentrated on rebuilding itself. In the countryside, as it gathered strength, there was a surge in rural terrorism: attacks on isolated police posts, kidnappings, intimidations.

On the whole, FPL personnel were busily training in the Soviet Union, Mexico, Guatemala, and Costa Rica as well as in Cuba. And this time there would be no mistakes, no overreaching. Those trained abroad in turn trained others back in El Salvador. Today's estimates of the FPL's manpower vary, but a strength of 800 to 1,000 combat-ready guerrillas is not farfetched. What's more, this hard core is backed up by some 2,500 tacit supporters. Leadership of the insurgency has tightened up. The FPL is directed by a tough, central group which, through harsh discipline and revamped security procedures, has had remarkable success in foiling penetration since the 1976 debacle. As a result, much is unknown about the actual size of its central command and its makeup.

Available facts suggest the FPL is organized into four regional committees based in the cities of San Salvador, San Miguel, Santa Ana, and Aguilares. The most important regional organization is buried deep within the capital of San Salvador. The regional organizations are subdivided into local committees which use classic cell structures to limit exposure of the cadres one to the other. This improves security and may explain why FPL action teams have been so successful in abduction and assassination operations.

Financing has been no problem. For example, one knowledgeable Mexican banking official estimated that from 1976 to 1978 the FPL gained more that $9 million in ransoms alone. A year later, a risk assessment expert, working out of London for an insurance company, concluded that in the first three-quarters of 1979 the FPL had accumulated more that $4 million through kidnappings. This same individual also acquired fragmentary evidence that the Soviet Embassy in Costa Rica is a conduit for funds going to the FPL. Indeed, the FPL is so comfortably in the black it could not only sustain its own operations but grubstake the Sandinista National Liberation Front of Nicaragua as well. In addition, reports from American businessmen working in El Salvador suggest that the FPL has given seed money to the revolutionary group in Guatemala known as the Army of the Poor (EGP).

Like its healthy cash flow, arms are rarely in short supply. The FPL has acquired an assortment of weapons through familiar insurgent methods—stealing from the Salvadorian forces, buying on the black market, and smuggling from abroad.

But the picture is even gloomier still. The FPL is not alone in El Salvador. Other insurgent groups are also in touch with Cuba. As it has noted increasing violence in El Salvador, political polarization, and U.S. timidity, Havana has become more willing to take political risks. Officials from Cuban embassies in Costa Rica and Mexico have dealt with a second Salvadorian terrorist outfit, the Armed Forces National Resistance (FARN), which probably numbers between 600 and 800 men. In addition, some of the leaders of the FARN, like Eduardo Sancho Castaneda, have visited Cuba for strategy discussions. During these sessions the Cubans have urged increased cooperation between the various insurgent groups and the Communist Party of El Salvador. Prior to events in Nicaragua, such advice went unheeded because of differences between the Communist Party and insurgents about when and how to stage the revolution.

As cadres in El Salvador studied the causes and consequences of Somoza's defeat, they realized that El Salvador is too small (2,400 kilometers) and too densely populated (4,515,000) to be a stage for a rural, Nicaraguan type of revolution. Instead, they elected to return to urban insurgency, using the vehicles of labor agitation and terrorism. With improved security, a trained combat force of 800 to 1,000 men, and a hodgepodge ideology of Marxism-Leninism and Maoism, the FPL was ready to try once again. It became bolder as this confidence grew. Assassinations were added to the wave of kidnappings. The unified Popular Liberation Army (FPLP) was hatched from cadre cells and guerrilla bands. Growth of their mass military power, according to FPL thinking, depended directly on how soon the Sandinistas in Nicaragua consolidate themselves and are then able to supply them with weapons on a large scale. Previously the FPL set no timetable for victory. But buoyed by the Nicaraguan experience, individual cadres have predicted the fall of the government by the end of 1980.

El Salvador, headed by President Carlos Humberto Romero, appeared in mid-1979 to recognize that social discontent has made open revolution less a possibility and more a certainty. But his government did little, if anything, to cope with political chaos. For want of a better policy, the president simply decided to hold free municipal legislative elections in March 1980 under international supervision. Political exiles were told they could return home to participate in this "democratization" process. The hope was that a civilian would become the next president and allow military leaders to return to the barracks.

This wishful thinking was challenged by those in the military who believed that such steps were only placebos and as effective in stopping social or political unrest as a BB gun might be in bringing down a rampaging elephant. As a result, even tourists in El Salvador during the summer of 1979 could not help overhearing rumors of a pending coup. Sure enough, their ears had not deceived them. With kidnappings, assassinations, and bombings by leftist organizations multiplying, there was a corresponding increase in lawlessness by the right. Anarchy was perceived by the military to be just one or two more murders away. A two-man junta decided to correct the situation. On October 15, 1979, it announced President Romero's ouster.

The apparent leaders of the coup were a Colonel Jaime Abdul Gutiérrez and Colonel Adolfo Arnoldo Majano. They quickly expanded the junta to a five-man body that included three civilians. But it soon became clear that the coup was really the handiwork of more junior officers who had organized themselves into a clandestine Military Youth Council. Predictably, the change of government did little to slacken the tensions. The militant left, including the FPL, lost no time in denouncing the coup as a maneuver designed to disguise the former government in sheep's clothing. Nothing, they said, had changed. Worse, many believed them.

In the first quarter of 1980 El Salvador was still in the incipient phase of insurgency, but the "war of national liberation" has since been nourished. In the coming months it is sure to expand. Much depends on the will of those who are now in power to meet the continuing challenges of change. Leaders favoring a democratic approach to the future face formidable odds in attempting to save the country from civil war, anarchy, and eventual Communist control. A full-scale Marxist revolution can engulf El Salvador at any time as the insurgency mushrooms out of the incipient phase.

What can be done to help El Salvador stay out of the Communist orbit? First, the government of El Salvador must field sufficient quick reaction forces to check the current wave of terrorism. Nothing can be accomplished without meaningful security. Yet, ominously, visitors note there is rarely a visible sign of authority when violence takes place. This impression of helplessness must be eliminated by the deployment of police and military personnel into potential troublesome areas. The stutter of submachine gunfire and the crack of explosives cannot go unanswered. Police and military communications desperately need improvement. Prompt grants of such equipment by the United States would be one way of helping a neighbor in need.

But muscle *must* be accompanied by an improvement of the country's political climate. Colonels and majors are not likely to accept democratic reforms and a true civilian rule until they see progress toward security and stability. The United States must accept this reality. But it should not act alone. Other interests are at stake here—for example, those of West Germany and Japan, whose products and technology have found eager markets in our hemisphere. Together, we should persuade the junta to develop a coherent program of reform. Some examples:

- A date for free elections.
- Unrestricted return of exiles to participate in politics.
- A church-state dialogue to enhance human rights and the social well-being of the populace.
- Financial pump-priming for urban and rural reform. This could be obtained from foundations, trade unions, or business interests in West Germany, Japan, and the United States.

Most immediately, the United States should assist Salvadorian authorities by applying tourniquets to arms-smuggling arteries from Nicaragua and Cuba. The two countries should also cooperate to penetrate terrorist groups, rendering them less effective. We have the tools and know-how. Time must be bought with which to accomplish social, economic, and political goals. A viable democratic center might emerge in the less violent atmosphere which would be created by reforms. If it did, extremism of both the left and the right could be contained and then reduced.

It is unlikely that El Salvadorian leaders, alone and unaided, can derail the revolutionary locomotive now gathering momentum. They must have U.S. help. From my own experience it is possible to estimate that the cost to the U.S. would not exceed $5 million a year. As for staff, no more than five intelligence professionals assigned full time would be needed. By anyone's measuring stick, this is a bargain. Consider the alternatives.

CHAPTER VI

OPERATIONAL PHASE

If, despite aggressive countermeasures, an insurgency is able to grow to multiple bands of twenty or more men in a single district or province, the movement has escalated to the next and most violent of all stages. Now the insurgency threatens the survival of the government itself.

In the operational phase, guerrillas surface to confront security forces in open combat. Their tactics are now more hit than run. The risk is often worth the gain. If they have accurately calculated their strengths—and government weaknesses—they can drive out security forces to the point at which authority must abandon the region, leaving guerrillas in sole possession of the population. If this falls short of the mark, they try at least to own the night. The tempo of recruitment increases. The delivery of arms by foreign importers or through raids on government installations reaches a feverish peak. Meanwhile, civic action and political indoctrination programs among the populace intensify.

The increasing aggressiveness of the guerrillas in the form of more frequent and large-scale assaults acts to open the desperate government's jugular further. Combat widens and escalates. But all caution is not thrown to the winds. To guard against the possibility of their forces being wiped out in one costly fire fight, the insurgent bands remain organized in separate units. However, they now—many for the first time—know of each other's existence. To maximize the impact of operations, they coordinate through clandestine communications—couriers, dead drops, meetings in safe houses, coded radio messages, and the like. The longer the guerrillas are permitted to operate at this level, the more they consolidate control over an area, the stronger they will grow. It becomes easier to receive fresh supplies, security is harder to pierce. Indeed, at this stage the guerrillas may have added antiaircraft weapons to their armory, endangering airborne or helicopter assaults by government forces. The flow of intelligence and recruits dramatically increases, for at least in this region they *are* the government—and the people know it.

Legal authority *must* respond promptly to defeat the insurgency lest it grow to an even greater danger. Here are the necessary steps which can still be taken at this late moment in the struggle by the central government and its American advisers—assuming, of course, they are on hand.

1. *Accurately determine the guerrillas' strength, disposition, and intentions.* Quality, timely intelligence is indispensable to the defeat of any guerrilla force. It can best be gathered from deep-penetration agents who have managed to have themselves recruited by the guerrilla bands. The difficulty does not lie in finding these assets. As the insurgency grows, guerrilla forces must run the risk that less reliable recruits will be attracted to the movement. For them the glamour may quickly fade as hardships in the bush increase. Enough sun, sweat, hunger, and fear can streak the most professional of makeups. And when it does, government talent spotters must be ready to pounce.

The real problem lies in receiving communications from such a double agent so he can warn the security service of his unit's next move. Inasmuch as guerrillas often move in remote areas, the problem is significant. Yet it can be solved with ingenuity and technology. Take, for example, a commercially available electronic device like the lightweight Narco Electronic Position Indicator Radio Beacon (EPIRB).[7] This is no whiz-bang

[7]Kent Richardson, "Saved by an EPIRB," *Yachting* (July 1979), pp. 111–13 and 124–26, describes how a sea-to-air beacon was used to rescue a small boat crew in the North Atlantic in October 1977.

gadgetry. It is simply a beeper which emits a steady signal as long as its tiny solenoid batteries have life. Ditched air crews use them to enable rescuers to pinpoint their location. Suppose such a device was inexpensively modified and installed into equipment which is permitted to fall into guerrillas' hands. The equipment could run from a first-aid kit to a flashlight. Suppose, then, that signals from such a device were picked up by an aircraft flying over suspected guerrilla base areas. Instantly the guerrilla unit's location would be pinpointed. The technique hardly requires a Merlin to pull it off. Nor does it need Midas. At present rates the device can be purchased for only $300. The more complex problem is how to exploit this tactical intelligence without exposing—and killing—the agent who furnished it. If one were to use the information to bomb the guerrilla camp, government forces might be bombing their own agent, for such weapons do not recognize passwords. A solution requires that the security service running the agent possess detailed knowledge of the guerrilla's environment and life in jungle camps.

Laos was one testing ground where American advisers combined just such a knowledge of the area with basic technology to avoid these dilemmas. As an example, let's take a look at a case in which basic details have been altered to protect those who were involved. A Meo, who was gang-pressed into a Pathet Lao unit, decided to use family connections to relay a message to a Meo irregular unit under the command of the royal Lao government's General Vang Pao. Contact was maintained with the agent in this manner until it was decided that more sophisticated means were called for. How, for example, were we to know where the guerrilla band—and an agent—were at any given moment? To this end a clandestine exchange of "walking sticks"* on a remote mountain trail was arranged.

The agent's "new" assault rifle, disguised as his own—down to chips and a reproduction of his hand carvings—contained a device which was the equivalent of the EPIRB beeper. From then on, the agent's signaling gear was no more than an arm's length away. Wherever it went, its giveaway transmission was as easy to spot as a shark's fin in a swimming pool.

By the monitoring of this beacon, movement patterns by the Pathet Lao were plotted. But our dilemma remained: How could our man be protected if an attack were to be launched against the group by air? When the options were discussed with the Meo penetration agent at a preselected jungle meeting site, an operational plan developed. The Meo, who was an animist, had adopted the habit—by now accepted by his Pathet Lao associates who were Buddhists—of morning communion with spirits he believed inhabited a clump of trees which grew a few hundred yards

---

*A walking stick is a staff that facilitates moving over a mountainous terrain. The Meo personalized these sticks with carvings and other hallmarks.

from the Pathet Lao base camp. It was agreed that a Union of Lao Races Radio broadcast in Meo would transmit a code word on an appropriate Wednesday evening broadcast. The code word, when heard by the agent on a transistor radio listened to regularly at the Pathet Lao camp, meant an attack would be made the next morning, weather permitting. Upon receiving his coded signal, the agent knew that he should proceed the next morning to his regular spot of worship but at the first sound of an attack flee into the jungle.

When weather was favorable, tactical aircraft were available, and signals from the beacon clear, the code word was broadcast. As the haze cleared off the mountains the following Thursday morning, two formations of three Royal Lao Air Force T-28 aircraft swooped down upon the camp. The six fighter-bombers caught the enemy by surprise, and their bombing and rocket fire caused massive secondary explosions as enemy fuel and ammunition supplies went up in every direction.

Weeks later reports trickling in from Pathet Lao prisoners confirmed that this attack had cost the guerrillas twenty dead, thirty-five wounded, and several munitions dumps. The destruction of the base camp was total. Having gained a head start, the Meo penetration agent escaped unharmed.

2. *Intensify counterintelligence operations against the guerrillas' support apparatus.* The secret supply lines through which a guerrilla receives food, medicine, and arms are perhaps his single greatest weak-

Operational Phase

ness—if security forces are sufficiently informed and equipped to shut them down.

As all roads once led to Rome, so do supply pipelines to an enemy's camp. This is as much a fact as a growling stomach. Assume that security agents learn that a particular peasant is found routinely larding a food cache near his village for the guerrillas. The agents then can slip a signal beacon into the supplies which will enable them— with proper U.S. equipment—to track the movement of these supplies to the guerrilla base camp. Once that occurs, a tombstone for the group is as good as carved. This technique was used successfully in Malaysia as late as 1974 to disrupt the activities of Malaysian Communist Party guerrillas who were operating as insurgents deep in the jungle.

3. *Devise psychological warfare operations to keep progovernment resistance alive in guerrilla-controlled areas.* If guerrillas control an area by night, the government should use radio and television to convey messages of hope aimed at persuading listeners and viewers that the guerrilla occupation is temporary. This must be done subtly so that the campaign does not propagandize for the guerrillas' cause by revealing government weaknesses. "We shall return," MacArthur said. And he did. No promises that cannot be kept should be made.

4. *Start an "open arms" program which appeals to the guerrillas to lay down their weapons in return for amnesty.* The open arms program must realistically show

insurgents what a brighter future can hold for them, their families, and the nation. For those who respond, it is critical that credibility be fortified by sending them to centers for vocational training and political reorientation. When the reeducation process is completed, the government should publicize success stories of guerrillas who have rejoined the government so that their former comrades-in-arms still in the bush can believe that their own defections can be beneficial.

The open arms concept was field-tested in Malaysia as the Surrendered Enemy Personnel Program and judged a success. It was later applied in Vietnam, where it convinced thousands of Viet Cong and some North Vietnamese to come over to Saigon's side each month. The sultanate of Oman has also experienced success with this technique in its struggle with the Popular Front for the Liberation of Oman (PFLO). The number of defections has not been great. Indeed, they range from one to two per month. But their quality has been impressive, and the absence keenly felt. A dividend is the self-doubt sown among guerrilla cadres: Who will succumb next?

5. *Expand civic action programs in the areas adjacent to those where the guerrillas dominate.* Civic action programs, begun in the incipient phase of an insurgency, should not be abandoned because the insurgency has reached the new plateau of its operational phase. Spread more health and economic opportunities to as large a segment of the popu-

lation as possible. The emphasis should be on programs which prove that cooperation with the government will pay off with better economic and social dividends than those the guerrillas offer. In Laos we found the use of bulls, imported from Thailand to improve the quality of the hill tribe herds, was an effective technique. This apparently insignificant gesture convinced the people that the government was in the war for the long haul.

6. *Step up the intensity of antiguerrilla operations by the elite antiguerrilla unit.* If organization of the elite antiguerrilla unit began in the cadre phase, as it should have, the unit should now be at its full strength of 550 men. It should be fully deployed in platoon formations against the twenty-man guerrilla bands. Superior equipment, training, leadership, and motivation will soon be felt.

A proved reality of irregular warfare is that guerrillas buckle under sustained pressure in their operational areas. If, acting on reliable intelligence, the antiguerrilla unit makes contact with an enemy unit in a raid, ambush, or patrol action, it must not relax its grip until the enemy surrenders or is defeated. Tactics are critical. Night-vision devices, helicopters, and gunships—plus advice from a one- or two-man American unit—can keep the enemy force pinned down or on the run. In either case, contact should not be broken. Better communications, mobility, and firepower will inevitably lead to the defeat of the individual guerrilla band. Each victory should be widely publicized in all the media throughout the country, for defeat is propaganda that guerrillas can ill afford.

Fidel Castro, having been a guerrilla himself, understood how best to deal with them. After the Bay of Pigs fiasco he applied these same tactics to destroy the Miami-based exile organizations that were operating as guerrillas in Oriente, Pinar del Río, and Camagüey provinces. By 1966 the last vestiges of meaningful opposition had been eliminated from those traditional areas where irregular warfare could be waged. Castro did this by ceaselessly pressing the guerrillas with large numbers of troops, who wore the guerrillas down until they had either to surrender or to stand and fight against superior forces. Cornered, the guerrillas were crushed.

7. *Establish population controls.* As guerrillas become operational, they normally must vanish from society, their homes and favorite haunts. It is at this point that population controls are needed, particularly in the districts adjacent to the guerrilla operating area. The key to a population control system is an identification document issued within a limited period of time to all residents of a given area. The card should exhibit a photograph, a fingerprint, and a basic description of its holder. And it should be tamperproof. A by-product of issuing the document is an accurate census of everyone living in the district. Suspicious shifts, increases or declines, can be quickly noted. Mean-

while, the guerrilla's movement is restricted. Without such a document he can scarcely run the risk of a check by security teams.

8. *Organize local self-defense forces.* A local self-defense force, or citizens' militia, should be recruited in the districts adjacent to the guerrilla operational area rather than in them. These forces are trained with light infantry weapons to defend their own villages, if or when the insurgency spills over.

If these forces are motivated, well led, and supplied with reliable communications equipment, they can be effective indeed. But more conventional forces should be kept close by to cover the local forces by artillery support or air power. A village protected by a tough self-defense force becomes a springboard from which government forces can mount their own offensive operations.

9. *Coordinate conventional military forces with the elite antiguerrilla unit.* When the presence of guerrilla units in an area, but not their exact location, is detected, sweep-and-encirclement operations are one time-tested way of finding and eliminating them. Conventional forces should carry out sweep operations themselves. Meanwhile, the elite antiguerrilla unit can take up blocking positions across likely routes to or from suspected guerrilla locations. As sweep operations get under way, the guerrillas will flush and slip away toward safe areas or their base camps. A nasty surprise will await them if the antiguerrilla unit has been prop-

erly positioned. Again, superior training, equipment, and firepower should smash the scattering guerrillas.

10. *Keep the enemy off balance.* Mount raids against sanctuaries or supply depots in nations bordering the operating zone. If the guerrillas are receiving logistics support or sanctuary from a neighboring country and if their depots can be pinpointed within ten kilometers of the border, hit-and-run commando raids should be launched against them. It is a high-risk and politically sensitive operation, and the raiders should be carefully chosen from regular military forces. The goal is to wreak as much havoc as possible among guerrilla personnel and to destroy a maximum of equipment. Such raids send a clear political message to the neighbor that is interfering in the internal affairs of another state.

In November 1979 South African forces killed seventy-five South-West Africa People's Organization (SWAPO) guerrillas and destroyed numerous weapons caches in a series of deep-penetration raids into Angola and Zambia. Prior to political settlement, Rhodesian (Zimbabwe) forces successfully attacked guerrilla bases in Zambia, Mozambique, and Angola. In hindsight, this concept may have been the single most important tactic used by Rodesia to keep the guerrillas off balance and incapable of realizing their full military potential.

11. *Establish an interrogation capability that can promptly exploit guerrilla prisoners.* Each revolutionary movement has its own jargon and idiosyncrasies.

Operational Phase

It is essential that the government train specialists who can speak the insurgent's language, recognize his weaknesses—in short, know him better than he knows himself.

In the mid- to late 1950s in Kenya, British interrogation teams literally wrote the book on how to conduct such interviews. Their skill and insight were primarily responsible for crushing the Mau Mau insurgency and paving the way for a peaceful transition to independence. The bonds which tied a terrorist to the movement were forged in superstition. Recruits underwent gruesome "oathing" ceremonies conducted by Mau Mau witch doctors. Not only did these sessions rob the recruit of his dignity and self-respect, but they also swore him to secrecy. Were he ever to betray the oath, it would kill him. This was fervently believed and was rooted deep in tribal custom. But the British found a shortcut. Interrogators simply hired their own "witch doctors," who, with appropriate mumbo jumbo, de-oathed the oath taken by the prisoner. Free of its stigma, the terrorist cooperated willingly. Together with sound knowledge of the guerrilla's personality and motivation, such skilled interrogations can rapidly extract intelligence from both prisoners and insurgents who have returned under the open arms program. Also, captured enemy documents can be better analyzed.

Interrogation should begin as soon as possible to take advantage of the captive's confusion or disorientation. Information should be exploited in a matter of hours, if possible. Otherwise, tactical advantages will vanish. The guerrillas will cover their tracks quickly once they discover the loss of either a cadre member or documents. Interrogation specialists must be both flexible and mobile. They must be prepared to move to where the prisoners are first brought in at a moment's notice. As time passes, the nucleus of expertise created in this phase can become a foundation on which to build a series of provincial interrogation centers that will support the government forces most heavily engaged in counterinsurgency operations.

This approach has been successfully utilized in Venezuela, Columbia, Malaysia, and the Philippines. It is essential for any serious commander of a professional counterinsurgency effort.

CHAPTER VII

WESTERN SAHARA
—A Case Study
of the Operational Phase

Few Americans know or care much about the guerrilla war that persists like flies in the forbidding, faraway deserts of the Western Sahara in northern Africa. Yet this forgotten insurgency today confronts our citizens with a serious challenge to their worldwide interest. Leaders in the Far East, the Middle East, Latin America, and, surely, the Kremlin are watching to see if, or how, we respond. Our response, or lack of it, will be interpreted as another indicator of what to expect from the United States in the 1980s.

The evolution of this particular guerrilla war illustrates why a great power cannot afford to remain oblivious to events in the rest of the world, no matter how much the power might wish to ignore them.

When the movement that was to blossom into a full-fledged insurgency originated in 1968, few parts of the world were of less concern to the United States than the 266,700 square kilometers constituting the Western Sahara—about the size of Colorado. The area, bordered to the west by the Atlantic Ocean, shoehorned between Morocco, Algeria, and the land now known as Mauritania, was under Spanish control. It was—and is—mostly desert, an anvil for a pitiless sun. Although it contains some valuable mineral deposits, it had few population centers. Only about 75,000 people inhabited these frightful wastes. And many of them were nomads, as though to remain in one place were to roast to death.

In 1968 Saharian students living in Rabat, Morocco, fell under the spell of the wave of nationalism then sweeping across Arab nations. They founded the Saharian Liberation Front, which opposed Spanish rule of their homeland. At first they only staged political rallies and wrestled with organizing a fledgling political base. Really, nobody cared less—least of all Spain. On June 17, 1970, however, they became news. In dispersing a demonstration in El Aaiún, the capital of Spanish Sahara, Spanish police overreacted and killed several onlookers. The mistake provided the Saharian Liberation Front with the one key ingredient they lacked: martyrs—symbols of injustice around which future supporters could rally.

The sparse population of the Western Sahara included a nomadic tribe, the Reguibat, who traditionally roamed over wide areas of northwestern Africa. Except for the ocean, the Western Sahara has no natural frontiers. Thus, the Reguibat ranged freely into Algeria, Morocco, and Mauritania. Hardy, proud, and independent, the Reguibat have learned to live off the land, to survive in a hostile environment, by adapting themselves to its climate and terrain like chameleons. They also are expert marksmen. Not illogically, it was to the Reguibat that insurgent leaders turned to recruit their first armed cadres.

The escalation of the insurgency beyond the cadre phase between 1970 and 1973 is shrouded in rumor. However, by 1973 the movement had surfaced and held its first political "congress," now called the Frente Popular para la Liberación de Saguía el Hamra y Río de Oro (Popular Front for the Liberation of Saguía el Hamra and Río de Oro). The title came from the region's natural zones: Saguía el Hamra in the north and Río de Oro in the south. The name was soon shortened to simply Polisario.

By 1973 the movement began to receive Soviet arms and support from Algeria and Libya. As if in repayment, it quickly assumed an increasingly anti-Western posture.

Resorting to classic guerrilla warfare, Polisario forces, composed mainly of the Reguibat tribesmen, started raiding Spanish outposts. After each raid the insurgents melted away and retreated to base camps in the desert, where superior knowledge of terrain gave them tactical advantage over their pursuers.

The assaults continued and inflicted painful casualties on the Spanish for the next two years.

Meanwhile, Morocco claimed that the Spanish Sahara belonged to its territory by historic right. It pressed the claim because of rich phosphate, uranium, and oil shale deposits known to be buried in the desert. Spain acknowledged that Morocco might have a valid claim to part of the Western Sahara, but not all. On November 14, 1975, prolonged negotiations culminated in a Spanish agreement to transfer joint sovereignty over the Western Sahara to Morocco and Mauritania. However, when Spain formally abdicated control and withdrew its troops in February 1976, it insisted that the Saharian people should have the right of self-determination. In other words, who was to rule whom?

Morocco argued that the right of self-determination was exercised that same month, when a majority of the Saharian Territorial Assembly voted to integrate the Western Sahara into Mauritania and Morocco. Accordingly, in April 1976, the two adjoining nations formally divided up the Western Sahara by announcing new boundaries. Morocco acquired the northern two-thirds of the Sahara, containing most of the mineral reserves, and Mauritania took the southern third.

But in this game of geopolitical monopoly, no one had included the reality of the Polisario. Its forces swiftly moved into the vacuum created by the departing Spanish. They were soon locked in combat with both Moroccan and Mauritanian troops, who discovered that the insurgents were deadly foes. The Polisario was able to field a force of between 3,000 and 5,000 guerrillas, composed mainly of the tough tribesmen and experienced veterans of service as Spanish territorials. Using Land-Rovers to increase mobility, they struck at Moroccan patrols, ambushed convoys, and mined supply lines. The net result: Thirty to fifty Moroccans were killed each month. But against the weaker Mauritanians, they mounted battalion-size offenses. In May 1977 they struck into Mauritania itself, besieging the town of Zouerate and damaging its ore-mining facilities.

But individual Moroccan troops also fought well, and when provided tactical air support by Mirage fighters, they hurt the guerrillas badly. By the middle of 1978 it seemed doubtful that the Polisario could graduate beyond the operational phase of insurgency, as a result of its limited manpower reserves and dependence on external supplies. Although they could not eliminate the insurgency, the Moroccans and their Mauritanian allies had contained it, albeit at the price of significant manpower and economic resources. The war became a standoff.

In July 1978 the scales tipped when a new government in Mauritania committed itself to ending the war. Not long after, its troops were ordered to abandon the Western Sahara. This allowed the Polisario forthwith to move in, set up new bases, and improve its logistic system. It also left Morocco holding the bag.

Morocco responded aggressively by withdrawing

troops stationed on reserve in Mauritania, annexing the southern third of the Sahara, and dispatching 15,000 to 20,000 men to hold it.

By now, however, the Polisario was given new life by the advantages of having to fight only a one-front war. Morocco stood alone. The guerrillas took the offensive. On January 28, 1979, they overran a sizable Moroccan population center for the first time—the town of Tantan. In August they routed the garrison of Lebuirate in southern Morocco and occupied that town. A Moroccan relief column managed to dislodge them within twenty-four hours. Nevertheless, attacks of this magnitude unveiled a new threshold of guerrilla capability—and a grave danger to the Moroccan government under King Hassan II.

A respected European political analyst calculated that by August 1979 the war was costing Morocco $350 million a year, minus its casualties. With neither a negotiated settlement nor victory in sight, Moroccan public opinion turned against the struggle. Such unrest could inevitably lead to the overthrow of King Hassan by a military coup.

By summer 1979 Washington policy makers, who had considered any exercise of American power in the Western Sahara unthinkable, began to think about it. The reasons were compelling.

In addition to being a man of great personal integrity, King Hassan is one of the most steadfast of Western friends. He is also loyally regarded by our few remaining allies on the African continent—not to mention Saudi Arabia. This is due to the fact that he has repeatedly demonstrated his convictions by courageous stands against more militant neighbors. His personal diplomacy, goodwill, and imagination were largely responsible for creating the climate for the secret Egyptian-Israeli dialogue which led to President Anwar Sadat's historic 1977 visit to Jerusalem and the subsequent Camp David accords. In April 1978, when former Katangan radicals invaded Zaire and endangered its copper mines and sovereignty, King Hassan sent Moroccan troops.* Their aid was decisive in repelling the invaders. In other ways which cannot be disclosed, Hassan's statesmanship and bravery have significantly benefited the United States and the West.

All this aside, King Hassan has steered his nation to democracy as rapidly as culture, tradition, resources, and political realities allow. In comparison with other regimes of the region, his has stood as a beacon of stability, progress, and hope. This does not mean additional reforms are not needed. Indeed, they are, and the United States should play a role in urging that they take place. His ouster would, however, leave the Moroccan people—as well as our own—with an uncertain and less promising future.

Although Hassan is not a puppet of the United States, or anybody else, he is correctly perceived as a leader who, because of his own beliefs and views about what is best for his people, has irrevocably cast his lot with the West. Should the United States fail to help him and his nation, we would be seen,

*So did the French—a clear lesson to a confused America of how to act when one's interests are at stake.

correctly, as having forsaken yet another loyal friend in time of crisis.

These were only some of the considerations that caused alarm in Washington. And they still do.

The insurgency in the Western Sahara and its threat to Western interests could not continue without substantial foreign assistance. The Polisario insurgents will have no incentive to negotiate meaningfully as long as they can rely on this assistance—unless of course the United States elects to give Morocco the means of defeating the insurgents.

Most of the military equipment and munitions obtained by the Polisario flow from Algerian depots kept well stocked by the Soviet bloc without restrictions on usage. Additionally, Algeria affords the insurgents sanctuaries and training sites and allows them to maintain a major base near the border city of Tindouf, where thousands of Saharian refugees congregate. They form a pool from which the guerrillas can replenish their manpower and strengthen their support mechanisms.

Algerian motives for providing this assistance are threefold. First, to exploit iron ore deposits in the Tindouf area, they wish to secure port facilities on the Atlantic by controlling the Western Sahara through a Polisario victory. Secondly, should Hassan's forces successfully absorb the Western Sahara and exploit its mineral reserves, they fear that Morocco would become a powerful rival. Finally, there is ideological animosity between pro-Western Morocco and Algeria. Though wary of falling into the Soviet orbit, Algeria is more inclined toward

East than West. On occasion it serves as a Soviet proxy, mostly to beard the lion in its own den—i.e., the West.

Support of the insurgency costs the Algerians comparatively little and gives them no cause to fear retaliation from the West. Thus, they see no reason to withdraw their support from the Polisario.

Similarly, Libya has learned that it can breed international terrorism and foment revolution as far away as the Philippines, the Caribbean, and Central America with impunity. So it, too, continues to provide Soviet arms and its own oil profits to the Polisario Front.

Morocco has charged that Cuba actively aids the insurgents. It is probably right. Evidence indicates that a group of approximately twenty-five guerrillas traveled via Paris to Havana for training in October 1976. Moroccan claims that Cuban advisers train Polisario members in Algeria and sometimes accompany them on combat missions in the Western Sahara have not been independently substantiated, so far as this writer knows. But as of late 1979 at least fifteen Cuban diplomatic and thirty-five medical personnel were known to be in Algeria. The presence of such an abnormally large Cuban contingent is certainly suspicious—unless, of course, there are a lot of sick Cubans in Algeria.

Indisputably Cuba has provided the Polisario Front with vigorous political and propaganda support in the nonaligned movement. Yet, while exhorting everybody else to recognize the Polisario's political front—the Saharan Democratic Arab Republic—Cuba has stopped short of granting such recognition itself. For although Castro desires to polish his image as revolutionary *extraordinaire*, he does not want to go so far as to lose the millions of dollars Cuba annually earns from sugar sales to Morocco.

The United States had three obvious choices as it muddled through its policy toward Morocco: It could remain passive and indifferent, thereby shunning an ally in peril and risking the fall of another strategic territory; it could use its good offices and those of its allies to try to promote a negotiated settlement between Morocco and Algeria; it could give Morocco the wherewithal to defeat the Polisario by providing it with professional counterinsurgency advice and equipment.

After the Mauritanian withdrawal in 1978 some of us in the U.S. intelligence community saw a need to protect Moroccan and our own interests. A debate of sorts ensued between strategists, mostly in the National Security Council and the Defense Department, who believed we should not risk offending the third world through any exercise of power, however indirect. Ambassador Andrew Young was a leading proponent of the latter view.

In a rather timid test of political waters, the Carter administration attempted to determine what the attitude of Congress would be toward sale of attack helicopters and reconnaissance aircraft to Morocco. Congressional attitude in 1978 was sharply negative. Rather than try to explain to Congress what was at stake, the administration shelved the idea of helping Morocco. Nothing was done.

Western Sahara

However, the developments of 1979 raised the issue anew and forced a reassessment which showed clearly that the restrictive arms policy had not benefited the United States. Harold H. Saunders, assistant secretary of state for Near Eastern and South Asian affairs, told the House Foreign Affairs Committee in July: "The Polisario's decision to increase the scope and intensity of the fighting had made it difficult for us to maintain Moroccan understanding for a U.S. arms policy of great restraint."

Still, the administration dithered in indecision until prodded by our Arab friends in September 1979. President Sadat publicly announced that Egypt was prepared to supply arms and aid to Morocco in the war against the Polisario. The Moroccan government, two days later, replied with a circumspectly worded expression of gratitude to Sadat and the fraternal Egyptian people.

American and other Western analysts read a deeper meaning into these diplomatic tea leaves. Their conclusion: Saudi Arabia—Egypt's bankers—had decided no longer to oppose aid to Morocco, even if such aid was American and was transferred through Egypt. A worried ally was sending a message to Washington: "Stand by your friends." Anxious to soothe the Saudis, who were both alarmed and disgusted by repeated displays of American impotence, the administration finally made a decision in October 1979.

It was to assist Morocco in achieving a negotiated settlement, rather than a military victory. Given this objective, the administration ruled out the dispatch of badly needed American advisers. President Carter, though, announced on October 22, 1979, that the United States would sell the Moroccans *limited* quantities of counterinsurgency hardware, principally Cobra helicopter gunships and armed reconnaissance aircraft, OV-10 Broncos.

By keeping to the middle of the highway, the President was run over by traffic both going and coming. The compromise satisfied neither those who favored decisive use of counterinsurgency skills nor those who opposed any intercession. Typical of the latter was Representative Stephen J. Solarz, chairman of the House Subcommittee on Africa, who declared the President's decision was "compatible with neither our principles nor our interests." Proponents of counterinsurgency were pleased at least to see a dawning awareness within the administration that tools, other than sledgehammers or opiates of self-delusion, are available to perform complex foreign policy tasks. They also welcomed the immediate relief the modest assistance will afford the Moroccans. However, they feared the decision will result not in an equitable negotiated settlement, but rather in a prolonged and ever more costly stalemate.

Still, at the beginning of 1980 it appeared that the United States could elect to do much more.

The Iranian revolution, with its resultant chaos and near anarchy, and the Soviet invasion of Afghanistan altered the strategic balance of power in the Persian Gulf and Indian Ocean regions against the United States. More important was the national and international humiliation the United States suffered in the eyes of its own people and the rest of the world. For the United States dramatically demonstrated that it was incapable of projecting power, conventionally or covertly, to rescue hostages held by a fanatical terrorist group. It was reduced to going ignominiously from one farcically ineffective international body to another, hat in hand, begging that someone else solve our problems for us. Even a gasoline station operator like Billy Carter became a go-between.

Pressures brought to bear by this degradation, coupled with alarm within the administration, compelled yet another reappraisal of basic foreign policy objectives. Moreover, the national psyche began to shed some of the self-imposed mental limitations that had so strongly influenced—some might say enfeebled—foreign policy ever since the Vietnam War. The administration pronounced a need to establish a mobile U.S. strike force, to reinstate draft registration, to prepare contingency support bases in Somalia, Oman, and Kenya, and to repeal or modify legislation which, in practice, had made major covert actions impossible. All these reflected a new awareness that it might be necessary to exercise power abroad. And one even heard expressions of the novel opinion, novel at least during the past decade, that should the United States exercise this power, conventionally or covertly, it ought to do so with a resolve to win.

Within this refreshing climate there exists the possibility that we may recognize that we ought to do much more to help Morocco promptly terminate the insurgency—either by outright victory or by forcing the insurgents to negotiate. This must be a national decision made not by intelligence or counter-insurgency professionals, but by elected leaders. This decision will no doubt be affected by the outcome of the 1980 presidential election. But policy makers should know that if a decision is made to assist Morocco meaningfully, the resources and professional techniques needed to implement this decision will need to be refurbished. Here are some timely steps:

- First of all, the United States should conceive and coordinate among all relevant government departments a comprehensive assistance program which integrates military, economic, and political considerations. This effort should have as a primary goal the creation of a climate of confidence in Rabat which would permit political, social and economic reforms to take place in a more timely manner.
- The United States should persuade Saudi Arabia to advance Morocco some $350 million for the purchase of an appropriate mix of American OV-10 reconnaissance aircraft, F-5 fighter-bombers, C-130 cargo planes, and attack helicopters. This combination of airpower would enable Morocco to search out the Polisario and inflict costly casualties. It also would deprive the Polisario of the ability to mass forces for attacks on Moroccan population centers.

  Given aircraft that almost ideally meet counter-insurgency requirements, Morocco could provide better tactical air support to ground units, thereby enhancing both their defensive and offensive capability. The cargo planes would permit better logistical and medical support to combat personnel. This, in turn, would measurably improve the morale of troops by assuring them better rations, frequent rotation out of combat areas, and, most important, lifesaving evacuation by air if wounded.

- With the goodwill that it would acquire through broader support of Morocco, the United States should persuade King Hassan to modernize the chain of command in his military establishment. Decentralization means commanders have more freedom to act quickly and flexibly. Air power, communications, and intelligence must be better coordinated. Collection and exploitation of intelligence must be improved. Photographic intelligence from tactical aircraft, use of infrared devices to find Polisario camps in the desert at night, and creation of relay centers to speed the flow of assembled intelligence to commanders in the field would be a great help.

- The Moroccans need foreign advisers to assist them in using new equipment and applying new counterinsurgency concepts. If the United States remains unwilling to lend American advisers, it should help covertly assemble qualified instructors from elsewhere.

- America should promote formation of an international consortium composed of France, Spain, Saudi Arabia, and itself to finance development of

Morocco's phosphate, uranium, and oil shale deposits. But in a display of evenhandedness, the consortium should make arrangements for Algerian iron ore to be transported freely through Morocco to an Atlantic port for export to world markets at favorable prices.

- America should concentrate upon persuading Algeria that continuation of the proxy war against Morocco is not in its national and strategic interests. Algerian concern over Libyan meddling in neighboring Tunisia, coupled with new incentives offered by the West, might make continuation of the insurgency difficult, if not impossible.

The foregoing program would cost money and manpower, although they would not have to be borne solely by the United States. The fundamental question policy makers must ask is whether the costs of doing nothing might not be far more.

CHAPTER VIII

COVERT WAR PHASE

Some mystery surrounds what point an insurgency shifts into top gear, its covert war phase. Like the tide coming in, the changes can be blurred, subtle. It creeps forward. Then, at once, you are in it over your head. The time has come for action—that is, if the United States wishes to have any say at all in the outcome. In any reading of the danger signals, there are several new characteristics to look for.

In the covert war phase the insurgents begin to coordinate their attacks in battalion stength, simultaneously in two or more large regions. Not always do they strike as a battalion, however. Often companies from these battalions will appear in different locations to harass government forces, to police the battlefield for weapons, and further to dramatize government weakness to those living nearby. By now the insurgents are able to fight pitched battles of prolonged duration against conventional forces and inflict heavy casualties. Elsewhere, neither the elite antiguerrilla unit nor conventional forces of the government are able to prevent the guerrillas from cutting vital railways and highways. The time has arrived when the government is no longer able to halt expansion of the insurgency with forces on hand.

The presence of a few advisers, a couple of dozen sophisticated aircraft, and limited amounts of other selected equipment will not help. Time is running out. Will the United States provide military equipment and other assistance on a large and diverse scale? Or do we pull back and write off another ally? Are we prepared to send American civilian or military personnel—or enlist qualified foreign personnel—to work with the besieged country's forces down to the company level? This is what will be required—but it need not mean the use of American combat troops. Rather, teachers of leadership and tactics and the use of more sophisticated hardware equipment are what is required.

Assuming we decide that it is in our best interests to prevent the beleagured nation's collapse, we should jointly do the following:

1. *Establish force levels for the government's conventional forces to be supported by United States equipment.* On the basis of a mutual intelligence

assessment of the threat, a joint force level should be agreed upon. The agreement should specify the total size of the force, its organization and equipment, and a timetable must be set for combat readiness. Usually the remaining time available will not allow us to reequip the nation's army fully. So both parties should concentrate on upgrading roughly a fourth of the country's forces. These, then, will become a spearhead against the insurgency which is now in full bloom.

2. *Provide an airlift capability, usually under commercial cover, to move supplies and personnel to staging areas.* Given the emotions in the third world, our target nation may wish to avoid the impression that it is being kept glued together by a Western power. There are valid reasons why the government may wish to soft-pedal such outside assistance. In this case, airlift under commercial cover is one effective disguise. In other words, let's invent an airline.

The unmasked aircraft should deliver American supplies directly to the regions where the forces are fighting, not to a central depot in the capital. This speeds delivery of equipment to those who need it most. It also cuts the hemorrhaging of material which can occur from a single arms dump.

But things are not that easy. An infrastructure to support the airlift must be built. Landing strips must be blasted out of dense jungle. Fuel bladders—they are just that, rubber and shock-resistant containers for kerosene and aviation gas—must be on hand to service the aircraft when they arrive.

And once prepared, the jungle strips must be protected. For, if they are to be of any use, they must be located near combat zones. And there is more yet. Crews must be prepared to parachute supplies—around the clock, if necessary—to government forces deep in the bush or cut off from relief. This means a careful mapping of the terrain and split-second timing between drop crews and troops on the ground. Only then can constant pressure be brought to bear on the enemy.

Outside of delivering tools of war, the airlift can provide medical services to the combat troops. Nothing will buoy morale more than certain knowledge that troops will be promptly evacuated to hospital facilities if they are wounded. The airlift, when not providing support to combat forces, can be used for civic action missions. For example, livestock can be delivered, along with building materials and farm machinery—to say nothing of med-evacing sick villagers for treatment. Such high-visibility civic action can be a push in the right direction to those who remain unconvinced of this government's determination not only to win the war but also to improve the lives of its citizens.

The record shows that the CIA's Air America provided just this kind of support to those fighting "wars of national liberation" in Laos and Vietnam. It did so with a fleet of short takeoff and landing aircraft—literally able to land on mountaintops—helicopters, and a fixed-wing armada of multiengine aircraft, such as the versatile C-123 and the workhorse C-130. Air America was both versatile and successful because it had a first-class assortment of deeply committed and professional crews.

3. *Furnish instructors to expand specialized military training programs.* When sophisticated equipment is supplied to conventional forces locked in a guerrilla war, lack of qualified training personnel limits their effectiveness. How, for example, can we expect a third world trooper—with a lack of educational skills—to instruct others in the use of devices like anti-intruder radars, night-vision optics, or remote sensors? One might as well provide them with bows and arrows.

This problem can be overcome only by qualified instructors from Western nations who can teach such specialties as demolition, disarming of booby traps, sniper tactics, and ambush defense. They need not be Americans, for qualified professionals can be recruited by the host nation with U.S. help from third-country governments. A few experts can triple the effectiveness of any training program. Preferably the training should be done in host country facilities. There are circumstances, however, in which the training must take place abroad or in nations close by. Here, then, is a place where we can borrow a page from the Kremlin's book.

A classic example of how foreign instructors can help build an effective fighting force began with a January 1961 contact by American personnel with a Meo leader, Vang Pao. An American paramilitary expert became convinced that Vang Pao and his Meo irregulars were determined to stay in the hills north of the Vientiane plain and resist the Communist drive which had swept across a large part of the Plain des Jarres. On the basis of the conclusion that Vang Pao would indeed put up a flight, coupled with American policy to contain the Pathet Lao, the CIA proposed to arm 1,000 Meo. This recommendation was approved in January 1961 by Assistant Secretary of State J. Graham Parsons, Admiral Harry D. Felt, Commander in Chief Pacific Forces (CINCPAC), with Headquarters in Honolulu, and Winthrop Brown, American ambassador to Laos.

By March of that year this force had expanded to 4,000 men. Understandably the CIA wanted to keep a low profile in Laos, so arrangements were made for members of an elite police unit from neighboring Thailand to help train the Meo. The Thai instructors taught the Meo map reading, tactics, demolitions, and the use of their American-supplied weapons. These irregular warfare experts were later enlarged by Royal Thai Army personnel. Without these instructors, Meo resistance, which started with 4,000 men and grew to over 25,000, would never have become a reality.[8]

---

[8]*Laos: April 1971*, a staff report prepared for the use of the subcommittees on U.S. Security Agreements and Commitments Abroad of the Committee on Foreign Relations, United States Senate (Washington: Government Printing Office, 1971), on page 15 identifies 39,000 irregulars in Laos in fiscal year 1969. It should be noted the Meo were an integral part of this total figure.

4. *Selectively employ "volunteers" as combat troops or advisers.* The supply of high-quality manpower is limited in any country, even less so in a besieged third world nation. Rather than stand by and watch these units bled white, the use of skilled volunteers should be considered. They can be elite combat units or advisers who accompany local forces in the field. Combat leadership is indispensable. How, then, to recruit them?

The volunteers can be reservists from a neighboring country who have just finished tours of active military duty and are hired to fight on fixed contract terms. Obviously their own government must be sympathetic and well aware of the dangers of the insurgency's becoming a threat to their own security. It is a wise idea, however, not to allow their friend-in-need to fall into the trap of relying on such aid—at the expense of shouldering its own defense burdens.

If properly devised and administered, volunteer forces can load the dice against insurgents. In June 1970 Laotian Prime Minister Souvanna Phouma appealed to the royal Thai government to send three additional army battalions to Laos. Souvanna planned to deploy them around population centers in southern Laos to counter increasing North Vietnamese and Pathet Lao attacks. He requested that the United States underwrite the Thai units as well as those that were already engaged in the fighting in North Laos. For policy reasons Thailand and the United States refused the request. Instead, a more flexible and mobile plan was suggested: Thai volunteers formed into CIA Special Guerrilla Units, seeded in South Laos trouble spots. All parties eventually agreed to this proposal.

Now Thailand is about as close to a free society as one is likely to get in modern-day Southeast Asia, and the Thais are very sensitive about keeping it that way. They are resourceful and tough. Indeed, if there is one thing that many of them like better than their national beer, it's a good fight. Once the word was out, the government had little trouble raising a whopping thirty battalions of "volunteers." As the men completed their training, they relieved Thai regular units at Long Tieng in North Laos. They had served there for more than a year, defending the Meo heartland. By mid-1971 all Thai regulars had been rotated out of North Laos. From then on Thai participation in the Lao war was on a volunteer basis.

Each of the fresh 550-man battalions was led by fifty officers from the Royal Thai Army. But the remaining 500 men were recruited from civilian life, primarily from among those Thais who had previous military service. Regular army personnel were required to resign before they joined their units. It was understood, however, that they would be reinstated without loss of benefits after they returned from Laos. The program developed a formidable combat force which made a major contribution to the defense of Long Tieng, General Vang Pao's headquarters for his irregular forces, and the heartland of Meo resistance. Meanwhile, Lao General Vang Pao fought his war of position and maneuver to keep two North Vietnamese divisions off balance in North Laos. Success was largely due to the professional fighting instincts of the individual Thai soldier, the leadership of General Vang Pao, and the sound approach by Lao, Thai, and American officials to what at first appeared to be a complex problem.[9]

5. *Appropriately expand from the operational phase earlier programs which are proved successes.* In the midst of a full-blown covert war it is unrealistic to focus on furthering innovation-stage programs. No time exists. Survival is what counts. Emphasis should be placed on improving existing programs. Here are some examples which U.S. advisers and government officials should consider:

- Continue to widen intelligence collection on guerrilla strengths, dispositions, plans, and intentions.
- Step up counterintelligence operations against guerrilla support operations.
- Do not relax psychological warfare operations that keep alive the spirit of resistance to the insurgents in guerrilla-held areas.
- Expand the open arms program to encourage less committed guerrillas to surrender under provisions of amnesty.
- Broaden the scope of the civic action programs,

[9]"Withdrawal of troops from Laos underway"—Bangkok *Post* (Bangkok, Thailand) November 18, 1973, provides a Thai perspective concerning Thailand's involvement in Laos.

functioning in areas neighboring those the guerrillas operate in or control by night.

- Keep hitting the insurgents in their base areas with small, elite antiguerrilla units. Use booby traps.
- Maintain population controls to read the movement of people and commodities, both in and out of guerrilla-held areas.
- Further strengthen local self-defense forces.
- Plan more combined operations in which the conventional forces continue to coordinate with elite antiguerrilla units.
- Intensify raids on insurgent supply depots across the border in neighboring countries which support guerrilla operations.

As in the earlier phases, success or failure will determine if the insurgency moves on to the next and final phase.

CHAPTER IX

ANGOLA—*A Case Study of the Covert War Phase, or the Shoe on the Other Foot*

Survival of the government depends on foreign mercenaries, 18,000 of them. Foreign technicians and administrators run almost all of the economy—the part of it that still functions. Foreign police and intelligence officers control security. The nation's ports, both sea and air, are operated by foreigners. The one real income producer, oil, is administered by one set of foreigners and protected by another whose nation also shares in the revenues. Yet this massive foreign intervention has not managed to maintain even minimal standards of living. Shops are bare; factories are shut down; roads revert to muddy trails; railroads are silent, motionless. In the bush beyond the cities and towns the countryside belongs to the guerrillas.

This is the reality of Angola today. It is the same reality Angolans knew seven years ago, except then they were economically better off. Only the roles have changed. Now the foreign troops surrounded in fortified enclaves and towns are Cubans, not Portuguese. As before, foreigners occupy the best housing. The only imported goods and food are from Cuba, East Germany, and the Soviet Union. Dissent and insurgency grow. The frightened government—now missing its former leader, Agostinho Neto, who died in a Moscow hospital last year—depends more and more on Communist cadres from abroad.

During the colonial era the Portuguese ran things and took the privileges. But then the country worked, and there was some degree of tolerance. To many Angolans it must seem that history has come full circle— with a vengeance. Yet there is one striking difference between 1974 and today. The group that presently rules Angola, the Popular Movement for the Liberation of Angola (MPLA), received powerful external backing when it was an insurgency. But today's anti-Communist insurgents have no significant support from abroad. While the Portuguese faced guerrilla forces supported by the Communists and others, the Communist-sponsored government of Angola faces strictly indigenous movements which must rely on their own resources.

Yet the most influential political force in the country is the insurgent movement, while the minority, held together by Soviets and Cubans, proclaims itself the government. This tragicomedy has pre-

Angola

vailed since 1975, when the Portuguese withdrew from Angola and left three guerrilla movements to settle their differences peacefully or otherwise.

The winner to date is the MPLA, originally an anti-Portuguese guerrilla movement, founded in 1956. During its entire history its power has sprung from the support of the 1.7 million strong Kimbundu tribe (about 27 percent of the populace) and the bulk of the country's 120,000 mulattoes (about 2 percent). Combining this with tissue-thin support scattered among the hundred or so other tribes in Angola, one could estimate that about 35 percent of the population are genuine backers of the MPLA. Since 1975 the MPLA has controlled the Kimbundu heartland in the north-central region and the major urban centers.

The second liberation movement, the National Union for the Total Independence of Angola (UNITA), formed in 1966 by Jonas Savimbi, wields influence in the southern half of Angola. UNITA's strength is the 2.3 million Ovimbundo tribe and elements of three allied tribes, the Chokwe-Lunda, Ganguela, and Ovombo. UNITA can count on the loyalty of about 45 percent of the total Angolan population.

The third revolutionary group is the National Front for the Liberation of Angola (FNLA), headed by Holden Roberto. The FNLA has concentrated its activities in the far north, where it is supported by the Bakongo, yet another major tribe. Unlike its two insurgent compatriots, the FNLA can count on little strength in other quarters. It represents less than 12 percent of the total population.

Predictably, there was little peace in January 1975, when Portugal turned the country over to a governing body from the three liberation movements that had fought against it. In November 1975, despite rumbles of mass trouble to come, Angola was granted full independence.

Little changed. Tribal and regional support remained the strength of each movement and continues to override either political or economic realities. In hindsight, no one should have been surprised by the fighting which erupted among the three groups in mid-1975.

It has continued primarily because the MPLA, confident of powerful Communist assistance, saw no reason to compromise, even though the other two groups represented a majority of the people. To understand this confidence, one need only look at the Cuban forces that have decisively shaped Angola's political evolution since the Portuguese left. Fidel Castro had at last arrived on stage center.

For more than a decade Castro had hustled the third world, trying to promote revolutionary kinship with movements in hopes they might profit from Cuba's experience and seize power through a rural insurgency. Castro's lessons, learned in the Sierra Maestra, were taught to anyone willing to listen. But Che Guevara's *Götterdämmerung* in Bolivia in 1967 forced Castro to change tactics. He gave more aid to established guerrilla forces and less attention to

Angola

founding his own. Castro had supported the MPLA from 1961 on. But the total force of Cubans advising the movement never exceeded more than a few hundred men. Only limited numbers of light weapons were supplied. MPLA cadres were trained, of course, and Cuban propaganda lionized Neto's struggle. The door swung open in the late spring of 1975. Castro, in consultation with the Soviets, decided in 1975 to expand his involvement in Angola as Portugal's own revolution and retreat from Africa accelerated. But there were two other considerations. First, Castro was convinced that the United States, in a fit of hand wringing caused by the agony of Vietnam, would no more intervene in Angola than it would return to Southeast Asia. Castro probably was aware that the United States was giving some help to the FNLA, but it was not significant enough to concern him. He knew the United States, while still at the table, had folded its hand. Moreover, he was confident he could count on the Soviet Union. Secondly, Castro believed that increased aid to the MPLA would bring it victory, thus dazzling and saying to the world that he could export a successful revolution as far away from home shores as Africa. What he sought most, of course, was an impeccable set of revolutionary credentials. What the Soviets wanted is less clear-cut. But their historical interest in mineral- and oil-rich nations with port facilities is certainly one clue. Another can be found in the strategic location of Angola. Fully three-quarters of the West's imported oil moves south from the Persian Gulf, rounds South Africa's Cape of Good Hope, then heads north up the West African coast toward Europe. The huge supertankers must pass within easy range of aircraft based in Angola. And it requires no Svengali to venture that such bases might be used to choke off the oil and to divide and disperse further Western naval forces which would have to protect these vital sea lanes. But there is yet another bonus.

Angola shares borders with both Zaire and Zimbabwe. Neither nation is exactly an ocean of calm. Also, from Angola, the Communists can infiltrate and support guerrillas in Namibia, to say nothing of South Africa, farther south. In other words, it is a handy springboard for expanding additional "wars of liberation" through central Africa. Thus, Angola is more than a pawn on the Kremlin's chessboard of geopolitics.

Castro began throwing dirt on the casket before the mourners had even departed. The Cuban military buildup began in September 1975, via air and sea. By late October 2,000 Cuban troops were in Angola—two weeks *before* Portugal formally granted independence on November 11, 1975.

At the same time Soviet naval forces took up positions from which they could threaten to block Western interference with Cuban supply routes across the South Atlantic from the Caribbean. A Kotlin-class guided-missile destroyer, a large landing ship loaded with naval infantry, and the Soviet navy's largest supply ship steamed into the Gulf of Guinea. Farther north, a modern cruiser and an oiler lay off the Guinea coast. TU-95 bombers were ferried to the airfield at Conakry, Guinea, from which they could cover the Cuban sealift. Another cruiser and two guided-missile destroyers patrolled farther north near Gibraltar. The navies of the West had no comparable forces in the South Atlantic. *Fait accompli.*

During the period of initial buildup the Cubans suffered heavy losses, so heavy that they were in danger of being overwhelmed by coordinated attacks by the FNLA and UNITA. Then they were routed and badly mauled by a South African thrust into Angola in November 1975. Recognizing an opportunity to punish the Cuban adventure, Secretary of State Henry Kissinger advocated substantial U.S. support to Savimbi and Roberto. But Kissinger's appeal fell on deaf ears in Congress. The recently passed Tunney amendment to the Intelligence Appropriations Bill expressly forbade funding for anything other than intelligence collection in Angola.

Thus assured that the U.S. would not interfere with vulnerable lines of communication and supply, Castro and friends immediately reinforced their expeditionary army. By November a massive air- and sealift landed 20,000 Cubans in Angola. These troops, plus a total U.S. withdrawal, reversed the tide of battle and sealed the doom of the FNLA and UNITA. Spearheaded by thunderous barrages of Soviet-supplied, truck-mounted Katyusha rockets and an umbrella of air support, conventional Cuban forces soon gained control of the battlefield. By February 1976 they had driven their opposition back to the bush.

Believing the situation well in hand, Cuba began reducing its forces in Angola between March and August 1976. Castro, it seemed, had gained a cheap victory. But he was in for a rude shock. Without Cuban troops to backbone their own less-than-disciplined forces, the MPLA soon began to lose control over wide areas of Angola. Pro-Western UNITA and FNLA insurgents, encouraged by the inflexible field manual "ready-aim-fire" tactics of government units, quickly reasserted themselves. In our parlance, the struggle—far from over—had only reverted to the covert war phase. By September 1979 Castro had to change pace in mid-stride and reverse the rotation of forces back to Cuba. Despite this—and the continuing help from the Soviet Union—the Angolan government is today no closer to defeating the UNITA insurgency than it was when this phase of the war began in February 1976.

Since the start of the covert war phase, UNITA has reorganized and regrouped. It does not defend fixed positions. Rather, it fights as a guerrilla force, conducting small-unit hit-and-run operations. These tactics are apparent in UNITA's literal control over the vital Benguela Railroad. This lifeline is the principal access from the sea to Angola's interior. It is also the funnel through which both commodities and export materials must move. Guerrilla raids have virtually shut it down. Meanwhile, more than 5,000 Angolan and Cuban troops have been tied down trying to protect it. To date, they have been unable to keep it open.

Elsewhere, Cuban and government counter-insurgency forces have been equally unsuccessful. Despite their best efforts, UNITA is able to maintain a guerrilla force of more than 18,000 men. Nor does it appear to have any problems recruiting more. The main obstacle is a shortage of quality weapons, especially light antiaircraft missles. UNITA commanders in the field also need better communications equipment to coordinate operations. Even so, the guerrillas have managed to deny the Luanda government full control over one-third of the country.

This continuing stalemate has embittered relations between the Cubans and East Europeans on the one hand and the Angolans on the other. By 1977 Cuban arrogance had cost them the respect of their Angolan allies. Their suppression of a coup against Neto in May 1977—they killed thousands of Angolans suspected of participation—seared many memories. Indeed, these sauntering revolutionary "heroes" and their *machismo latino* are seen more as occupiers than supporters by an increasing percentage of the Angolan population. Just who are the colonials anyway? many ask. In such a charged atmosphere, 18,000 Cuban troops and Soviet tanks and aircraft and other supplies have been unable to help Luanda take the offensive.

The government has to content itself with periodic probing actions designed to keep UNITA off bal-

136

ance. And it is about as effective as a swimmer kicking at a circling shark. Cuban ground troops venture out of their garrisons much less frequently than they once did. They have even threatened to kill ten MPLA soldiers for every Cuban killed by the enemy, claiming that the MPLA flee the field, leaving them to die fighting UNITA. This valor in discretion may also be due in part to the caliber of soldiers the Cubans now send to Angola. Formerly most were experienced reservists; now they are raw draftees. But even the reservists, recalled to Angola after already completing one tour of service, had major morale problems. Moreover, the distinction of serving in revolutionary Africa has lost some of its former luster. Too many Cubans have been there. Returning "heroes" are thus greeted less by admiring *señoritas* than by a yawn and a "so what?"

Nobody wants to die in Angola, not anymore. Even the cream of the crop, Cuban combat pilots, is having second thoughts. Rather than scream in at tree level, where napalm, cannon fire, and rockets have their best effect on guerrilla concentrations, they now prefer to deliver such ordnance from increasingly higher altitudes—well out of the range of ground fire. Accuracy, to say the least, is haphazard.

Cuba's manpower losses so far are hard to calculate. UNITA claimed that 1,000 Cubans were killed in combat between September 1975 and July 1977. Cuban estimates, obtained through sources in Miami, place the figure at 600 for the same period. More neutral observers, however, have claimed that

Angola

up to 2,000 Cubans were killed between the fall of 1975 and the fall of 1978. This is the same per capita ball park figure as American casualties in Vietnam. These grim statistics caused some alarm in Cuba, but—unlike Vietnam—neither they nor the financial burden of the war pose a serious threat to Castro's regime. Unlike Presidents Johnson and Nixon, Fidel is not faced with the pressures generated by a free electorate and a skeptical Congress.

Given the control he exerts at home, and the luxury of lavish Soviet logistics, Castro can persist in trying to build the Angolan army, the FAPLA, into a modern force of 30,000 to 50,000 troops. UNITA, although broadly backed by the population, can only continue to fight in the bush. Its weapons and supplies restrict its growth to the covert war phase. Therefore, UNITA struggles on as best it can, hoping it will eventually force Luanda to make major political concessions. On the other hand, Luanda's prospects for a real victory are bleak. A stalemate is likely, since the MPLA and its Communist allies are firmly opposed to any concessions.

The death of Agostinho Neto has, if anything, lessened the chances of serious negotiation. The vacuum of leadership may touch off a new power struggle among his followers but is not likely to change either the MPLA's Marxist orientation or its alliance with the Soviet Union and Cuba.

Neto's succesor, Soviet-educated José Eduardo dos Santos, lends an aura of legitimacy to the new regime, because Santos was left in charge of the government when Neto went to the Soviet Union for cancer surgery in the summer of 1979—never to return. He may temporarily control external jockeying for power, but he will not significantly change MPLA's policies or the determination of UNITA to oppose them.

This stalemate in slaughter deeply affects the future of both central and southern Africa. Zimbabwe, Namibia, and, in fact, all the surrounding nations (which, among other things, are the world's greatest storehouses of critical minerals for the industries of the future) will certainly be influenced by what happens in Angola. If Angola were to expel Communist mercenary forces, the leftist political thrust of whole regions would be fundamentally changed. So we must ask: Should the United States help to resolve the Angola conflict or should we simply accept the status quo? But how could we promote or influence negotiations when we have no leverage? In our dilemma perhaps we could covertly—and decisively—support UNITA with what it needs most: weapons and advice. But this appears unlikely. The Carter administration, through its former UN ambassador and the assistant secretary of state for Africa, endorsed the Cuban presence in Angola as "a stabilizing force" on numerous occasions. As for the White House, the President did not dispute these shocking opinions by his subordinates. Far from it. According to the official view of the State Department, the Cubans protect Angola from South African incursions.

In November 1979 Jonas Savimbi himself visited the United States and told Congress that he was winning the war against the Cubans. No one acted. Meanwhile, South Africa suspended its clandestine support to UNITA in 1977 because it saw the insurgents needed more help than it could or should make available. Only France kept its lines open to Savimbi and provided UNITA with limited amounts of weapons and supplies through airlifts from Morocco. That is not enough to change the military balance. Only decisive action by the major Western powers can break the stalemate. Otherwise, Angola will be afflicted by insurgency indefinitely.

Instead of neglecting the festering struggle, we should look to our national interests and those of the majority of the Angolan people and weigh how they may benefit us both. Our support of UNITA and the FNLA might well push the government into serious negotiations. Certainly, nothing else is likely to do so. Beyond that, the covert war in Angola should have one objective: inflicting as many casualties as possible on Cuban forces. If Cuba can be made to pay a painful price in Angola, it might reconsider its role as a cat's-paw for Soviet military ventures in the third world. If that goal were achieved, it would blunt the Soviet plans to isolate the United States in a world which responds only to the Kremlin's wishes.

If they felt assured of a lasting commitment, UNITA and the FNLA would quickly grasp the significance of such a victory. The United States could join with France—were it willing—to provide basic Soviet-made equipment such as AK-47 assault rifles and deadly ground-to-air missiles like the SA-7.

These would decimate Cuban attack helicopters and thereby immobilize Cuban troops even further. As these weapons are in the Angolan government's inventory, courtesy of the Soviet Union, UNITA and FNLA could obtain spare parts, ammunition and replacements by simply capturing them. This would ease the logistics burden. Providing the insurgents with a modern communications system would improve coordination within guerrilla organizations and help them take the offensive against the MPLA and the Cubans. This covert war support would cost the United States about $10 million in equipment a year. Its supervision would require the services of only fifteen professional counterinsurgency experts.

At this point the cost of failure would be minimal. But success could reverse the whole course of history in Africa. Imagine a Cuban Dien Bien Phu, Castro's foreign legion surrendering and being escorted as prisoners back to the docks at Luanda. This third option is worth consideration, something to think about when one sees the placards of the Iranian militants on TV, the ones that say, "THE U.S. CANNOT DO ANYTHING."

CHAPTER X

CONVENTIONAL WAR PHASE

The final phase of a "war of national liberation" is reached when guerrilla forces decide their military strength is sufficient to confront government forces in a decisive battle. By this time there is little point in mourning the spilled milk of what went wrong for the government during the insurgency's earlier stages. The dilemma for the government is very simple: Either it survives, or it does not. It is no longer confronted by bush guerrillas. It must deal with an army. The insurgents now have such luxuries as long-range artillery and antiaircraft weapons. And they know how to use them. Ask the French, who, in 1954, hoped to suck Viet Minh "guerrillas" into a meat grinder called Dien Bien Phu.

French paras and legionnaires at Dien Bien Phu were not defeated by unconventional warfare. They were crushed by a superior force that employed superior weapons. Cut off from ground supply routes, they were forced to rely on airdrops. Then these, too, failed as pilots were forced to run a deadly gamut of flak from the hills surrounding the valley. Meanwhile, long-range artillery—firing from hidden positions—hammered at French hedgehog positions until, one by one, they were flattened. What was left was quickly overrun.

Can nothing be done to avoid a defeat of this magnitude? If it begins to appear the guerrillas might win the key battle, thus the war, the United States must reassess its own commitment. There are two options still available. The first is to abandon the counterinsurgency program entirely. This is a painful option, for it resurrects the unpleasant specter of defeat. Emotion, rather than logic, frequently plays a key role. Does one simply "write off" our losses already taken in trying to contain the insurgency in its earlier stages?

It is difficult—when one examines a program which may have been in operation for two years, perhaps even longer. For many who were responsible for its birth, the agony is not unlike that of watching a child die. Careers and reputations are seen to be at stake. Then, of course, there is politics. Who's to blame? Not I. If a meaningful appraisal of our position is to be made, there can be no bones to pick, no blame to fix. Hand wringing is pointless.

Conventional War Phase

Recognition of these dangers will help make for a more dispassionate and realistic analysis. Such a review must depend heavily on the judgment and experience of professional counterinsurgency experts. Their advice should be heeded. Otherwise, one might just as well ask an apprentice plumber to adjust the flow of water over Niagara Falls. Most dangerous of all would be to have the reappraisal conducted exclusively by political appointees. If left to their own devices, their lack of experience and hidden loyalties could easily cloud or influence a decision—perhaps disastrously. The prudent approach, therefore, would be to create a mixed panel of experts and political appointees to conduct the assessment. The product of their efforts should provide recommendations to elected officials on how to proceed.

Inevitably the second option arises: Is the United States prepared to intervene with conventional military forces? This choice was exercised in both the Dominican Republic and Vietnam. One was successful; the other became a national catastrophe. Clearly the national prestige of the United States is now on the line. Before taking this fateful step, we must weigh the consequences of not taking it. What, for example, will be the effect on our allies and on the Kremlin? How will they react? Every action—or lack of it—has an equal and opposite reaction. Take Israel, for example. Suppose it were about to enter negotiations for a West Bank settlement. Good faith hinges on a U.S. promise to support Israel in the event the settlement is violated and it is attacked. If that support is questioned, why should Israel negotiate seriously? A fool, they say, is quickly parted from his money—or his country.

NATO partners, jittery over American indecision, decide to assume a more concessionary posture vis-à-vis the Soviet Union. And who can blame them? They are considering *their* interests, their survival minus U.S. reliability. And so it goes. A house of cards without an ace. These are but a few of the considerations we should make in deciding whether or not to intervene actively in saving our threatened ally. Keep in mind that we have already spent many years doing just that. And like it or not, the United States is now part and parcel of that nation's survival.

Assume, then, that we consider the cost of doing nothing too great. The President and an informed Congress commit our conventional forces. Once done, there can be no turning back. There can be no alternative to victory in a conventional war in a third world setting against nonnuclear powers.

Thus, when the decision to intervene has been made, the conduct of the conventional war becomes the responsibility of the Department of Defense, which controls both the tactical and the strategic resources needed to achieve victory. At that point the insurgency has shifted from the covert to the conventional phase, and there must be a passage of the field marshal's baton from the CIA to the senior American military commander in the field. This exchange of responsibility must be accompanied by the prompt and unequivocal implementation of a new command relationship agreement. There can be no murkiness about who should do what, for war is intolerant of those who are not prepared and disciplined. Any lack of clarity in a combat command concerning who is responsible for what invariably translates into battlefield casualties, which no commander wants.

This transition to military control is easier said than done. The "old hands," no matter how hard pressed they and their guerrilla forces are because of enemy successes, suffer an understandable reluctance to give up command and control of their war to the "green" newcomers. At the same time the incoming military command, no matter how eager it may be to achieve success (and it is eager), is a bit unsure of itself because of its newness to the theater of war. It looks to the "old hands" for guidance and assistance. This is normal. In view of this, a transition period of up to ninety days may be needed to handle the smooth shifting of gears. All parties must keep in mind, however, that it is during this time of change that new operational policies tend to become entrenched. It is important to understand, therefore, that if decisions adopted during this period of adjustment, for expediency's sake, are "off the mark," they will haunt the command from that day forward until they are changed. The command relationship agreement is, therefore, a critical document to the success of the conventional war. All parties must give it their full support, particularly during the critical transition period.

The command relationship agreement, when it is invoked, must clearly define the roles of the ambassador, the senior U.S. military officer in the field, and the CIA. While a sensible command relationship evolved in our last war, Vietnam, there is a need to learn from this experience. A key conclusion which emerged was that there should be preparations *in advance* for potential wars that will see our paramilitary cadres relinquishing command over a covert war to the defense establishment as the war moves into a conventional confrontation. This is a crucial area of neglect which merits immediate attention by Pentagon planners, the State Department, and the CIA.

When this problem is solved and properly codified, the concepts inherent in the solution must be taught at the National War College and similar institutions attended by large numbers of State Department and CIA officers. Only through this approach will our new doctrine be sufficiently disseminated to those who may have to implement it during the 1980s.

After the conventional war option is selected, new relationships also have to be forged between arriving United States military commanders and the host country military establishment. This adjustment can be relatively problem-free, for many senior and mid-level officers from the host government have more than likely attended such training centers as Fort

Conventional War Phase

Benning or Fort Leavenworth. They know the conventional military system in the United States and how to work with it. As of now, a useful command relationship between the U.S. military and its foreign counterparts is easier to achieve than solving the same problem within our own establishment.

As the command lines are restructured, a concept of how best to conduct the conventional war must be agreed upon. The only choice here is the one-war theory. This doctrine grew from America's experience in Vietnam. Its strength lies in simplicity. All host government agencies must contribute to winning the war by a total reshaping of their missions to one goal and only one goal: taking the battle to the enemy. This means that intelligence and security officials, and their American advisers, must place their resources at the timely disposal of the military commanders. Essentially they are subordinate to the conventional military structure. But that is precisely what is required in the conventional war phase of dealing with a former insurgency.

In the one-war theory, host country intelligence and security forces, aided by their American advisers, should concentrate on:

- Producing positive intelligence of high quality on the strength, location, plans, and intentions of the enemy's military and political forces. What's more, the information *must* be timely if it is to be of use to the host country and the American military command. The operations planner (G-3) and the intelligence officer (G-2) must be informed about the enemy. Obviously this data will result in effective conventional operations against the enemy's forces.

- Mounting counterintelligence operations designed to protect United States and host country military units in the field by identifying, neutralizing, or manipulating the enemy's intelligence agents and their collection capability.
- Establishing escape and evasion capabilities using host country personnel operating behind enemy lines as guerrillas. The mere existence of such a force will contribute significantly to the morale of both American and government forces. In Vietnam, dramatic rescues of downed American and South Vietnamese aircraft crews by helicopter rescue units and irregular forces occurred time and time again—even in the heart of North Vietnam.
- Developing a resistance movement behind enemy forces. In addition to collecting intelligence, such teams can harass the enemy through low-cost, high-visibility sabotage operations. Examples: sniper attacks; booby traps. Thus, if the enemy wants to maintain security of his rear areas, he must tie down more and more manpower and equipment—all are assets that would normally be deployed against us in direct combat.

My debriefing of German soldiers who fought in Russia during World War II convinced me that destruction of military facilities and railroads by partisans was only a small part of the total impact of these guerrilla forces. More important was the fear Soviet partisans sowed among German troops. As the fear increased, German morale decreased. Nowhere did it seem they were safe.

- Utilizing irregular forces developed from the elite antiguerrila units to launch high-intensity raids and ambushes against enemy forces scattered in areas near the combat zones. For maximum impact these operations should be coordinated with attacks by conventional forces. The objective of these combined operations is to tie down enemy forces in flank security tasks, to lower morale, and to bleed off personnel from units fighting our conventional forces.

  In World War II the Soviets mastered this art of combined operations. German units retreating from massive Soviet frontal assaults often found their escape routes closed by partisans. This technique needs greater emphasis in U.S. military planning. Despite the Vietnam experience, deep-seated frictions and resentment—often jealousy— exist between our own conventional forces and elite commando units like the Green Berets. Yet both are in being to help the other.

- Mass psychological warfare operations designed to keep alive the flame of resistance throughout society. This can also help maintain stability within the host country government and its military forces in a time of great stress.

These steps are not sufficient in themselves to turn the tide of battle, but they are an indispensable part of the larger effort. Whether this formula produces

150

The Third Option

success or not, the first principle of conventional war
is that once the United States commits its national
prestige through its conventional military establishment against a second- or third-rate power, it *must*
pursue that decision to its logical conclusion—the
military defeat of the enemy. Anything less than
military victory cannot serve United States national
interests.

This raises the question: Can the United States
face the cruel reality of conventional war? Does it
have a choice? One could ask where on earth are we
likely to have to commit our conventional forces to
engage an insurgent enemy grown strong enough to
threaten an independent ally. Where? How about
the oil-rich Arabian peninsula? In other words, how
dispensable is Saudi Arabia?

Having posed the question and operating on the
premise that counterinsurgency has as its fundamental aim the prevention of conventional war, let's examine a futuristic scenario. South Yemen, aided by
its Soviet and Cuban allies, launches a covert paramilitary war against North Yemen. This war would
be fought by the tribal nomads living in both countries, with South Yemen using its Soviet-supplied
heavy weapons, superior communications, and logistics to gain the tactical advantage over North Yemen's irregular forces. In response to a deteriorating
battlefield situation, North Yemen urgently requests
American assistance. Saudi Arabia, seeing an immediate threat to its interests in a Yemen dominated
from Aden, uses its substantial influence in Washing-

ton to endorse North Yemen's request. The United States response is swift and effective—weapons, communications, and the CIA's counterinsurgency experts are brought into the covert war. South Yemen's previous tactical advantage is eliminated. The prospects are high that what will unfold is a long-term war of attrition.

Moscow decides, however, that its interests cannot tolerate a stalemate in Yemen's covert war. The battlefield escalation that flows from that judgment is both quick and decisive. Cuban troops enter the struggle in company- and battalion-size formations. North Yemen's tribal forces are routed. Its regular forces fare no better. Defeat is imminent. Sana, Riyadh, and Washington assess the situation in terms of what is to be done next. During these deliberations the retreat of North Yemen's forces permits the war to spill over into Saudi Arabia. Serious concerns are raised in European capitals and in Japan about Riyadh's and Washington's ability to stop the expansion of the war.

The options narrow. The basic question becomes: Does the United States help the Saudis push the war back into Yemen, or does Washington risk losing access to 9.5 million barrels of Saudi oil per day? The answer is pragmatic—commit America's rapid deployment force and support it from bases in Oman, Somalia, and Kenya to carry out a quick surgical operation to defeat South Yemen's forces that are in Saudi Arabia and North Yemen. As the Pentagon moves to put the genie of South Yemen back in the

152

bottle, the previously worked-out command relationship agreement permits an orderly transition of responsibility for the American involvement in the war from the CIA to the appropriate military commander. Once that is accomplished, the one-war concept is implemented as previously described.

Antiterrorist operations provide some of the same procedural challenges to American policy makers as does a conventional war. In my judgment a mobile strike force of conventional but specially trained infantry must be committed to the important mission of rescuing American hostages who are victims of terrorism. This function must also be assigned to the Defense Department, for when this force is committed to action, as it was in the abortive April 1980 attempt to rescue American hostages from Iran, the prestige of the United States is on the line.

Fixing the responsibility for such antiterrorist responsibilities with our military establishment is not a unique American phenomenon. The West Germans used this approach in Mogadiscio, Somalia, the Israelis at Entebbe, Uganda, and the British deployed their Special Air Services commandos to clean out the terrorists who took over the Iranian Embassy in London in May 1980. The factor that separates these foreign operations from our own is . . . success. They achieved it. The United States military did not when it attempted to rescue the hostages in Iran. One can conclude, therefore, that while our structural approach toward handling this task was correct, we fell short on implementation.

This presents us with the challenge of how to do it right. One answer is specialization. A small unit—a battalion—needs to be dedicated to nothing but hostage rescue operations. This unit should have the best of intelligence, air, and logistics support. Here, again, there is need for a command relationship agreement to handle the integrated task force that should be established as each hostage situation develops. The intelligence support for this task force should come from all national and departmental sources. The task force should, for the time that it is in existence, have its own intelligence staff which is an integral part of the task force. This type of integrated task force mechanism does not now exist. This is one reason why we have failed where others have succeeded. If this country is to achieve the success in the war on terrorism that has been attained by our allies, we must learn from the lessons of the past in order to cope with the future.

CHAPTER XI

THE BOTTOM LINE

Preceding chapters have outlined concepts for dealing with "wars of national liberation" through the timely application of American counterinsurgency techniques. They have been field-tested in the unforgiving school of two decades of practical experience. The counterinsurgency methods presented have also been appraised by a panel of experts I brought together informally after my retirement. In the year that we have met in small groups for seminar types of discussions, these twelve experienced foreign policy experts with extensive service in diplomacy, intelligence, the armed forces, media, academia, national-level politics, and defense-related aspects of the private sector have dissected and endorsed all aspects of the concepts outlined in this book.

Emerging from our hours of debate is the suggestion the United States may be ready to shed the paralyzing legacy of Vietnam and the more recent policies of noninvolvement in nations like Angola, Nicaragua, Iran, and Afghanistan. The group concluded that the United States cannot limit national security solely to military and political terms. The challenges and dangers of the 1980s require a great nation to view its national security in terms of the interrelationship among political, economic, and military factors—that is, if it intends to remain a power at all.

It seems to me that the counterinsurgency roles detailed in this book harmonize with what appears to be a reemerging American sense of values concerning the projection of power overseas. If so, then appropriate use of low-cost, high-impact covert action programs to achieve foreign policy objectives to help friendly nations resist subversion by the Soviet Union, Cuba, or China will receive the support of the American body politic.

But any future use of the third option presumes that the United States will be assured an uninterrupted flow of high-quality timely intelligence. It also assumes that intelligence will be objectively interpreted and analyzed, no matter how unpleasant its implications.

The United States cannot expect adequate intelligence without achieving a better balance in collecting it. One look at the intelligence budget, however, reveals that collection through satellites and other technical systems has been the centerpiece of recent funding. Indisputably these systems have performed brilliantly and can be expected to be equally rewarding in the future. But the question remains: Is the national collection system in its entirety adequately balanced between technical and human source activities?

Unhappily the answer can be found in the events that led to the 1979 debate in the United States over the presence of a Soviet combat brigade in Cuba. Surveillance satellites and electronic eavesdropping, skillfully employed, spotted the unit and established its capabilities. But these systems could not reveal how the Soviets or Cubans planned to use the brigade. While analysts could fashion scenarios as to why the Soviet brigade was in Cuba, they could not substantiate them. Thus, senior officials lacked critical intelligence on which to make far-reaching foreign policy decisions. The analysts simply lacked sufficient hard facts to decipher Soviet or Cuban intentions. This can come only from human sources—agents "in place" within either the Soviet or Cuban establishments, preferably both. The hue and cry about the Soviet brigade, touched off by disclosures made by former Senator Richard B. Stone of Florida, revealed that such intelligence simply did not exist. There was no such void in October 1962 when agents first revealed the presence of Soviet missiles in Cuba—and told us where to look to find and photograph them. The result was a national triumph of worth; absence of such intelligence led to a devastating humiliation in 1979.

This recent performance results from a lack of emphasis on human sources during Admiral Turner's stewardship of the Central Intelligence Agency and the intelligence community. To see just how low a priority has been assigned to such "assets," Congress needs only to reexamine funds (in constant dollars) and manpower allocated to agent operations. It also should examine the priority assigned Cuba on the national collection scale and study the results. Such a survey would lead Congress to some meaningful conclusions about the pitiful state of American intelligence—conclusions that the most artful or devious politician could not rationalize.

Nor is this all. Future use of the third option also depends upon the existence of a professional, highly motivated organization to undertake covert action and counterinsurgency missions. The CIA's clandestine service once provided just such an organization. But it has largely disintegrated. This deterioration did not take place overnight. It was a slow and painful process. Contributors to the demise were numerous—the media, congressional committees, special interest groups in the executive branch, and former employees like Philip Agee. The single most crippling blow, however, can be dated October 31, 1977, when Admiral Stansfield Turner, President Carter's newly appointed director of the CIA, ordered the so-called Halloween Massacre, eliminating 820 professional and semiprofessional positions in the clandestine service. He ordered the purge to accelerate dismissals and forced retirements, thus achieving his goal of reducing the size of the service. But he threw the baby out with the bath water. He succeeded in destroying employee morale throughout the CIA.

A reasonable case could be made for personnel reductions, given the reduction imposed on collection, counterintelligence, and covert action in the post-Vietnam period. What troubled the CIA's senior managers and employees most, however, was Turner's failure to grasp the significance of the human factor that is such an integral part of a well-balanced intelligence organization. In a professional sense, this is unforgivable. Employees knew that substantial reductions had been taking place in the clandestine service since 1969. But this had been done selectively, while our primary assets were retained. Equally obvious, further reductions, even of the magnitude that Admiral Turner decreed, could just as easily have taken place through a combination of attrition and the weeding out of unproductive personnel by their peers.

Rejecting this compassionate solution, Admiral Turner forfeited the confidence and respect of a large majority of our intelligence officers. A devout Christian Scientist, Turner is a decent man dedicated to serving his country as best he knows how. And surely no one can rise to the rank of full admiral in the U.S. Navy without ability. Yet Turner's actions caused him to be *perceived* in the eyes of the men and women of the CIA as a calculating, impersonal systems analyst who did not comprehend that his most vital resource was, is, and will remain *people*.

Whether these perceptions were justified or not, their effect was devastating. They resulted in a mass exodus of critical personnel from the clandestine service. More harmfully, they destroyed the esprit de corps, the traditional can-do spirit of those who stayed. But this was only the beginning.

Far from improving this self-destructive image, Turner only reinforced it. Because of personal differences with an outstanding clandestine service officer who had made some of the most significant intelligence contributions of the past decade, Turner personally denied the man a promotion to which he was indisputably entitled. The officer thereupon requested early retirement, which had been routinely granted to others of far less distinction. Turner denied the request. The officer thereupon quit in disgust. He told me after I had retired that he was unwilling to serve under the admiral for even eighteen months, which would have entitled him to a lifetime of full retirement benefits.

Such incidents appalled not only senior executives but junior officers as well. The youngest reasoned that if men of such standing in the service could be treated this way, so could they. This was further compounded by the admiral's habit of awarding key positions to those who shared one common characteristic with him—a lack of in-depth experience in intelligence.

For example, the deputy director was selected from the ranks of State Department ambassadors. A

Social Security Administration official was hand-picked to become the agency's chief administrative officer. An elderly professor quit a quiet campus to forge a new Foreign Assessments Center. A retired general from the Army Corp of Engineers was hired to develop an organization to coordinate intelligence collection missions within the intelligence community. These individuals were men of substance and accomplishment in their own fields. But they had little intelligence experience. No organization could accommodate this cumulative infusion of inexperienced talent—unless, of course, our few remaining agents abroad suddenly became instructed in bridge building, getting a doctorate, or filing for an old age pension. These weaknesses, coupled with Turner's own shortcomings, did not create a management team at the CIA equal to the challenge of the late 1970s and early 1980s.

Not suprisingly people continue to leave the CIA in droves. They, together with those who had been forced out, represented a priceless national asset—in experience and expertise that cannot soon be replaced. Berlin during the 1950s, Laos, the Congo and the Caribbean in the 1960s, Vietnam in the 1970s—all forced a rapid maturing of officers who served there. In many cases, one became a professional—or one became dead. Whatever the case, we accumulated a Midas' treasure of experience. Today young officers have no comparable proving ground on which to gain the field experience that is the basis for both sound judgment and creative innovation.

The wonder is that the CIA retains as many able people as it does. But if a signficant improvement in morale does not take place by late 1980, there will have been more than three years during which intelligence officers have become used to keeping their heads below bureaucratic parapets rather than take the bold risks often required in the collection and action arenas. This may well become the most devastating of Turner's legacies. For as those who follow become better able to judge his stewardship through the passage of time, they may find it necessary to credit him with the single-handed long-term destruction of the agency's spirit. This is something that the Soviets never accomplished, nor did the Church or Pike committees in their ideological and political assault on American intelligence.

The hemorrhage of talent from within the clandestine service has crippled the CIA's once-formidable paramilitary capabilities. Although President Carter approved a Special Coordinating Committee recommendation in November 1977 that the CIA should retain such a capability, Admiral Turner has continued to whittle away at the unit where just these skills exist. Professionals have resisted this steady erosion, fighting to keep on hand a minimum of trained personnel who could provide the expertise required by the third option. Additionally, some efforts have been made to add modestly to stocks of basic infantry weapons and ammunition so that a counterinsurgency could be sustained for at least six months if need be.

The Bottom Line

But Admiral Turner was far from comfortable with the presidential decision to maintain our paramilitary capabilities. In an attempt to find a rationale for abandoning it altogether, he created scenarios for its use, then ordered subordinates to prepare position papers on how paramilitary skills and supplies would apply to these problems of the future. His scenarios looked at problems such as: Could Yugoslavia be helped via American paramilitary skills to keep the armored might of the Soviet Union out of the country for a prolonged period in a sustained war in the post-Tito era? This, despite the fact that he claimed to understand that Yugoslav guerrillas could not hope to win a war of attrition against a superior Soviet conventional army. Other think pieces dealt with the topics: Could CIA personnel be brought out of the halls of Langley to run a *Guns of Navarone* commando raid on key military targets? It was difficult for the admiral to comprehend that CIA paramilitary experts were not soldiers or commandos. They were skilled organizers of insurgency and counterinsurgency operations to include recruiting, training, and logistics planning. These men always worked through local leaders and did not furnish combat leadership for indigenous troops. The end result was that Turner's scenarios were so far removed from world realities that subordinates concluded he either was obtuse or wanted to convince them to junk the CIA paramilitary capability as unworkable.

Conviction kept the CIA's professionals doing

what they could to preserve counterinsurgency assets, despite Admiral Turner's lack of support. In an attempt to justify the capability—and the option—decisions were made to use paramilitary officers to provide:

- Antiterrorist training for other agencies, both here and abroad.
- Assistance to the Defense Department in developing its own unconventional warfare capability.
- VIP protection training for third world nations—particularly in Africa and the Middle East.
- Support for intelligence collection tasks where there exists a need to field-test equipment or new delivery techniques.

This life-support system has preserved a limited paramilitary capability on a highly cost-effective basis. But it has *not* saved enough human resources to justify confidence that the United States could exercise the third option. To arm the nation with the capability to invoke that option—and to ensure the flow of intelligence essential for survival in the 1980s—the entire American intelligence community should be restructured.

Here are some positive steps which can be taken at once:

- Order a better balance between technical and human source collection.
- Restore a confidence between the American

people, the executive branch and Congress, and the intelligence community, on the one hand, and foreign liaison services, on the other.

· Develop new ways of conducting our collection, counterintelligence, and covert action missions to avoid damage by congressional investigations, executive branch malaise, media exposés, leaks, and release of sensitive information through the Freedom of Information Act.

· Convince Congress to create a single joint oversight committee for the intelligence community rather than the present stew of committees and subcommittees. There are eight in all. Obviously secrets are hardly safe—to say nothing about meaningful guidance and oversight when they are placed in escrow with multiple custodians.

· These goals can best be achieved by a Cabinet-level post of director of national intelligence (DNI). This new Cabinet member would be the President's personal intelligence officer, sitting and working in the White House as a coequal of the national security adviser. The DNI would be responsible for establishing collection priorities and requirements. He would also draft the intelligence community budget, defend it before the Office of Management and Budget, sell it to the President, and coordinate its movement through the Congress. He would also manage an Intelligence Community Staff that would coordinate the entire United States intelligence effort. The DNI would not, however, have any command and control over the running of CIA operations. He would also have no role in the writing of national estimates.

- Reestablish the President's Foreign Intelligence Advisory Board (PFIAB) to function as the nation's ombudsman for intelligence.

- Finally, the boldest step of all—do away with the CIA and create a new agency, the Foreign Intelligence Service (FIS). This new organization would retain all the CIA functions that did not pass to the DNI. In brief, it would be the nation's primary center of analysis and would be responsible for preparing coordinated national estimates. It would collect clandestine intelligence abroad and conduct counterintelligence and counterinsurgency operations. It would also be responsible for the protection and debriefing of defectors and the control of deep-penetration agents—or moles, popularly—who have managed to infiltrate adversary governments, military establishments, or secret services. If the new agency is to be effective, its director should be appointed for a six-year term in office, thus spanning two administrations.

The need for this restructuring of American intelligence has been brought about by such diverse factors as:

- Significant expansion of the fiscal and human resources committed to intelligence since the passage of the National Security Act of 1947.

The Bottom Line

- Increased complexity of technical systems, such as satellites, microwave intercepts, and U-2 reconnaissance planes, which are needed to collect capabilities intelligence.
- Experience, since 1947, proving that no director of the CIA has ever successfully been the President's personal intelligence officer, the coordinating manager of the intelligence community, and the chief executive officer who runs the CIA. In short, the span of control needed to fulfill these three tasks has eluded the grasp of talented men. This is persuasive evidence that the scope of responsibility for this position needs to be reduced.
- History has unfortunately treated the name "CIA" unkindly. A cosmetic change for America's premier service appears in order, therefore, if for no other reason than to shed a name that has served the nation well, but, in so doing, has become tarnished.

The reorganization proposal which I have outlined is not a master plan for the future of American intelligence. It is simply a skeletal framework which shows how counterinsurgency can relate to the broader issues of national interests. What remains to be done is to correlate this framework with the functions and missions of other intelligence agencies, such as the National Security Agency, the National Reconnaissance Office, and the FBI. In so doing, the nation can create a new intelligence structure for the 1980s. Such issues are beyond the scope of this book.

Congress has before it, however, the unique opportunity to spark those actions that will give America once again a solid first line of defense through its intelligence apparatus. What is at issue here is the country's survival. Sink or swim. It's as simple as that, really. Stripped of our power to influence events abroad—those, at least, which threaten our critical interests—we remain unprepared for the challenges of the 1980s. We must remember that in the end it is self-interest—not self-expression—that will preserve our great democracy.

In the final analysis, however, the bottom line on the decision to use or ignore the third option will not be based solely on the quality of intelligence, analysis, or oganizations. This decision will be made by those who have, or lack, the will to pursue policy goals through techniques that have preserved our interests in diverse areas such as Oman, Malaysia, the Philippines, the Dominican Republic, Venezuela, Bolivia, and Thailand, just to cite a few success stories. That will seems to have been rekindled in the land. Thus, one can conclude that in the 1980s we will see the third option become an integral part of the arrows that are in the nation's quiver of national security options.

Or should the nation settle for war?

BIBLIOGRAPHY

BOOKS

AKBAR KHAN, MOHAMMED. *Counter-Guerrilla Warfare.* Karachi: Rangrut, 1967.

ARNOLD, H.J.P. *Aid for Developing Countries.* London: The Bodley Head, 1962.

AYERS, BRADLEY EARL. *The War That Never Was.* New York: The Bobbs-Merrill Company, Inc., 1976.

BARRON, JOHN. *KGB. The Secret Work of Soviet Agents.* New York: Reader's Digest Press, 1974.

BARRON, JOHN and PAUL, ANTHONY. *Murder of a Gentle Land.* New York: Reader's Digest Press, 1977.

BAYO, ALBERTO GIROUND. *150 Questions for a Guerrilla.* Translated by Hugo Hartenstein and Dennis Harber. Boulder, Colorado: Panther Publications, 1963.

BEALS, CARLETON. *Great Guerrilla Warriors.* Englewood Cliffs, New Jersey: Prentice-Hall, 1970.

BITTMAN, LADISLAV. *The Deception Game.* Syracuse, New York: Syracuse University Research Corporation, 1972.

BLOODWORTH, DENNIS. *An Eye for the Dragon.* New York: Farrar, Straus and Giroux, 1970.

BUTLER, OLIVER J. *The Guerrilla Strategies of Lawrence and Mao: An Examination.* Houston, Texas: Butler, 1974.

BYAS, HUGH. *Government by Assassination.* New York: Alfred A. Knopf, 1942.

CASSERLY, GORDON, MAJOR. *Jungle and River Warfare.* London: T.W. Laurie, Ltd., 1914.

CLARK, GERALD. *The Coming Explosion in Latin America.* New York: David McKay Company, Inc., 1962.

CLUTTERBUCK, RICHARD L. *Guerrillas and Terrorists.* London: Faber and Faber, 1977.

CRASS, JAMES ELIOT. *Conflict in the Shadows. The Nature and Politics of Guerrilla War.* Garden City, New York: Doubleday, 1963.

DACH, HANS VON. *Total Resistance.* Translated by Hilary Sternberg, Boulder, Colo.: Panther Publications, 1965.

DANIEL, JAMES and HUBBELL JOHN G. *Strike in the West.* New York: Holt, Rinehart and Winston, 1963.

DEBRAY, RÉGIS. *Revolution in the Revolution? Armed Struggle and Political Struggle in Latin America.* Translated from the author's French and Span-

Bibliography

ish by Bobbye Ortis. New York: MR Press, 1967.

DIXON, CECIL AUBREY and HEILBRUNN, OTTO. *Communist Guerrilla Warfare.* New York: Frederick A. Praeger, 1954.

DON, TRAN VAN. *Our Endless War Inside Vietnam.* San Rafael, California: Presidio Press, 1978.

DONNEN, ARTHUR J. *Conflict in Laos, The Politics of Neutralization.* New York: Frederick A. Praeger, 1964.

DOW, MAYNARD. *Western Nation Building in Southeast Asia.* Boulder, Colo.: Pruett Press, 1965.

DRAPER, THEODORE. *Castro's Revolution, Myths and Realities.* New York: Frederick A. Praeger, 1962.

ELLIOT-BATEMAN, MICHAEL. *Defeat in the East: The Mark of Mao Tse-tung on War.* London, New York: Oxford University Press, 1967.

ELY, LOUIS B., COLONEL. *The Red Army Today.* Harrisburg, Pa.: The Military Service Publishing Co., 1951.

FAIRBAIRN, GEOFFREY. *Revolutionary Guerrilla Warfare: The Countryside Version.* Baltimore: Penguin, 1974.

FARER, TOM J. *War Clouds on the Horn of Africa: A Crisis for Detente.* New York: Carnegie Endowment for International Peace, 1976.

FELIX, CHRISTOPHER. *A Short Course in the Secret War.* New York: E.P. Dutton and Co., 1963.

GALULA, DAVID. *Counterinsurgency Warfare, Theory and Practice.* New York: Frederick A. Praeger, 1964.

GEYER, GEORGIE ANNE. *The New Latins.* Garden City,

New York: Doubleday and Co., Inc., 1975.

GIAP, VO NGUYEN. *People's War, People's Army.* New York: Frederick A. Praeger, 1962.

GOUDALL, BRIAN BRADFORD. *Revolutionary Warfare in South East Africa.* Johannesburg, South Africa: The South African Institute of International Affairs, 1966.

GREENE, T.N., LT. COL. (RET.). *The Guerrilla—and How to Fight Him.* New York: Frederick A. Praeger, 1962.

GRIFFITH, SAMUEL B., BRIGADIER GENERAL (RET.) (ED.). *Mao Tse-tung on Guerrilla Warfare.* New York: Frederick A. Praeger, 1961.

GRIVAS, GEORGE. *General Grivas on Guerrilla Warfare.* Translated by A.A. Pallis. New York: Praeger, 1964.

GRUNDY, KENNETH W. *Guerrilla Struggle in Africa. An Analysis and Preview.* New York: Grossman, 1971.

GUEVARA, CHE. *Guerrilla Warfare.* New York: Monthly Review Press, 1961.

GUILLEN, ABRAHAM. *Philosoply of the Urban Guerrilla: The Revolutionary Writings of Abraham Guillen.* Translated and Edited by Donald C. Hodges. New York: Morrow, 1973.

HAGGERTY, JAMES EDWARD. *Guerrilla. Cadred in Mindanao.* New York: Longmans, Green & Co., Inc., 1946.

HALBERSTAM, DAVID. *The Making of a Quagmire.* New York: Random House, 1964.

HALL, RICHARD. *The Secret State.* New South Wales: Cassell, Australia Limited, 1978.

Bibliography

HANRAHAN, GENE Z. (ED.). *Chinese Communist Guerrilla Warfare Tactics.* Boulder, Colo.: Paladin Press, 1974.

HARAKABI, YEHOSHAFAT. *Fedayeen Action and Arab Strategy.* London: Institute for Strategic Studies, 1968.

HEILBRUNN, OTTO. *The Soviet Secret Services.* London: George Allen & Unwin, Ltd., 1956.

HEILBRUNN, OTTO. *Partisan Warfare.* New York: Frederick A. Praeger, 1962.

HEILBRUNN, OTTO. *Warfare in the Enemy's Rear.* New York: Frederick A. Praeger, 1964.

HOANG VAN THAI. *Some Aspects of Guerrilla Warfare in Vietnam.* Hanoi: Foreign Languages Publishing House, 1965.

HYDE, DOUGLAS ARNOLD. *The Roots of Guerrilla Warfare.* London: Bodley Head, 1968.

JENKINS, BRIAN MICHAEL. *The Five Stages of Urban Guerrilla Warfare: Challenge of the 1970's.* Santa Monica, California: Rand Corporation, 1971.

JENKINS, BRIAN MICHAEL. *An Urban Strategy for Guerrillas and Governments.* Santa Monica, Calif.: Rand Corporation, 1972.

JOHNSON, CHALMERS. *Autopsy on People's War.* Berkeley and Los Angeles, Calif.: University of California Press, 1973.

JOHNSON, KENNETH F. *Guerrilla Politics in Argentina.* London: Institute for the Study of Conflict, 1975.

JURELDINI, PAUL A. AND OTHERS. *Casebook on Insurgency and Revolutionary Warfare; 23 Summary Accounts.*

Washington, D.C.: The American University, 1962.

KERR, ALFRED E. *The Art of Guerrilla Fighting and Patrol, A Manual of Infantry Defensive Training.* London: Jarrolds, 1940.

KY, NUGYEN CAO. *Twenty Years and Twenty Days.* New York: Stein and Day, 1976.

LABIN, SUZANNE. *The Unrelenting War.* New York: The American-Asian Educational Exchange, Inc.

LAGUEUR, WALTER. *Guerrilla: A Historical and Critical Study.* London: Weidenfeld and Nicolson, 1977.

LEVY, BERT. *Guerrilla Warfare.* Boulder, Colo.: Panther Publications, 1964.

LOCKWOOD, RUPERT. *Guerrilla Paths to Freedom.* Sydney, London: Angus and Robertson, Ltd., 1942.

MAJUMDAR, B.N. *The Little War. An Analysis of Guerrilla Warfare.* New Delhi: Army Educational Stores, 1967.

MAO TSE-TUNG. *On Guerrilla Warfare.* Translated by Samuel B. Griffith. New York: Frederick A. Praeger, 1961.

MARCOS, FERDINAND E. *Notes on the New Society of the Philippines.* Manila: Marcos Foundation, Inc., 1973.

McNAUGHTTON, WILLIAM (ED.). *Guerrilla War: Mao Tse-tung, Che Guevara, Sun Tzu, Chuko Liang.* Oberlin, Ohio: Crane Press, 1970.

OSANKA, FRANKLIN MARK (ED.). *Modern Guerrilla Warfare.* New York: The Free Press of Glencoe, 1962.

PENKOVSKIY, OLEG. *The Penkovskiy Papers.* New York: Doubleday & Company, Inc., 1965.

Bibliography

POSTGATE, RAYMOND. *How to Make a Revolution.* London: The Hogarth Press, 1934.

PYE, LUCIAN W. *Guerrilla Communism in Malaya.* Princeton: Princeton University Press, 1956.

RAUF, MOHAMMED A. JR. *Cuban Journal.* New York: Thomas Y. Crowell Company, 1964.

REISCHAUER, EDWIN O. *Beyond Vietnam: The United States and Asia.* New York: Vintage Books, 1967.

SCHANCHE, DON A. *Mister Pop.* New York: David McKay Company, Inc., 1970.

SELZNICK, PETER. *The Organizational Weapon—A Study of Bolshevik Strategy and Tactics.* New York: McGraw-Hill Book Co., 1952.

SHAPLEN, ROBERT. *Time Out of Hand.* New York: Harper & Row, 1969.

SHAPLEN, ROBERT. *The Road from War.* New York: Harper & Row, 1970.

SMITH, EARL E.T. *The Fourth Floor.* New York: Random House, 1962.

SMITH, JOSEPH BURKHOLDER. *Portrait of a Cold Warrior.* New York: G.P. Putnam's Sons, 1976.

SZULC, TAD and MEYER, KARL E. *The Cuban Invasion.* New York: Ballantine Books, 1962.

TANHAM, GEORGE K. *Trial in Thailand.* New York: Crane, Russak & Co., Inc., 1974.

THAYER, CHARLES WHEELER. *Guerrilla.* London: M. Joseph, 1963.

THOMPSON, SIR ROBERT. *No Exit from Vietnam.* New York: David McKay Co., Inc., 1969.

THOMPSON, SIR ROBERT. *Peace Is Not at Hand.* London: Chatto & Windus, 1974.

THORHOFFEN, ALEX (ED.). *The Citizen's Guide to Guer-*

rilla Warfare. Pasadena, California: Technology Group, 1976.

TRAGER, FRANK W. *Why Vietnam.* New York: Frederick A. Praeger, 1966.

TRINQUIER, ROGER. *Modern Warfare—A French View of Counter-Insurgency.* New York: Frederick A. Praeger, 1964.

ZASLOFF, JOSEPH J. *The Pathet Lao Leadership and Organization.* Lexington, Massachusetts: Lexington Books, 1973.

UNITED STATES CONGRESSIONAL PUBLICATIONS

COMMITTEE ON ARMED SERVICES, UNITED STATES SENATE. *Bombing in Cambodia, Hearings before the Committee on Armed Services July 16, 23, 25, 26, 30; August 7, 8, and 9, 1973. (Ninety-Third Congress, First Session).* Washington: Government Printing Office, 1973.

INDEX

Catalog

If you are interested in a list of fine Paperback
books, covering a wide range of subjects
and interests, send your name and address,
requesting your free catalog, to:

McGraw-Hill Paperbacks
1221 Avenue of Americas
New York, N.Y. 10020

Shackley, Theodore

The third option